D0195947

THE PRICE OF TAMING A RIVER

THE DECLINE OF PUGET SOUND'S DUWAMISH/GREEN WATERWAY

**Timberland
Regional Library
Service Center
415 Tumwater Blvd SW
Tumwater, WA 98501**

THE PRICE OF TAMING A RIVER

THE DECLINE OF PUGET SOUND'S DUWAMISH/GREEN WATERWAY

BY MIKE SATO

THE
MOUNTAINEERS

Published by
The Mountaineers
1001 SW Klickitat Way
Seattle, WA 98134

© 1997 by Mike Sato

All rights reserved

1 0 9 8 7
5 4 3 2 1

No part of this book may be reproduced in any form, or by any electronic, mechanical, or other means, without permission in writing from the publisher.

Published simultaneously in Great Britain by Cordee, 3a DeMontfort Street, Leicester, England, LE1 7HD

Manufactured in the United States of America

Edited by Paula Thurman
Map by Kristy L. Welch
Cover design by Patrick Lanfear
Book design by Alice Merrill
Page layout by Sandy Wing

Cover photograph: *Top*, The Green River at Orillia (photo by Mike Sato); *Bottom*, The Duwamish River south of Harbor Island (photo by Ken Lans)
Frontispiece: Duwamish Waterway at Harbor Island (photo by Ken Lans)

Library of Congress Cataloging-in-Publication Data

Sato, Mike.
    The price of taming a river : The decline of Puget Sound's Duwamish/
Green Waterway / by Mike Sato.
       p.   cm.
    Includes bibliographical references.
    ISBN 0-89886-490-9
    1. Water—Pollution—Washington (State)—Duwamish River
Watershed. 2. Water—Pollution—Washington (State—Green River
Watershed (King County) 3. Economic development—Environmental
aspects—Washington (State)—Duwamish River Watershed. 4. Economic
development—Environmental aspects— Washington (State)—Green River
Watershed (King County) 5. Pacific salmon—Effect of habitat modifica-
tion on—Washington (State)—Tacoma—History. 7. Duwamish River
(Wash.)—Regulation— History. 8. Green River (King County, Wash.)—
Regulation—History.   I. Title.
TD224.W2S281997
333.91'13'09797—dc21   97-12101
                                                CIP

♻ Printed on recycled paper

Contents

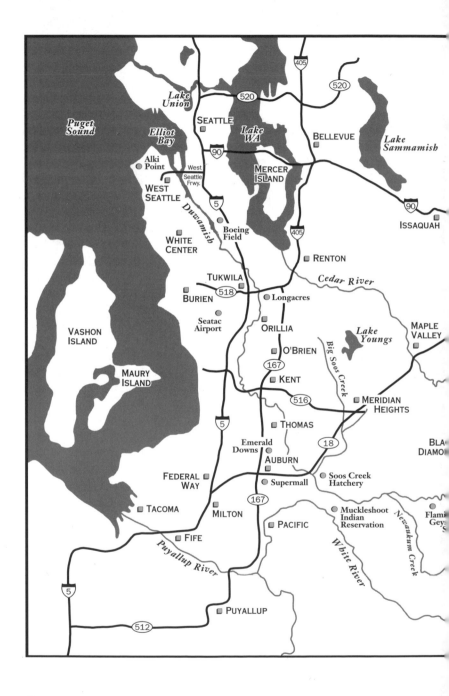

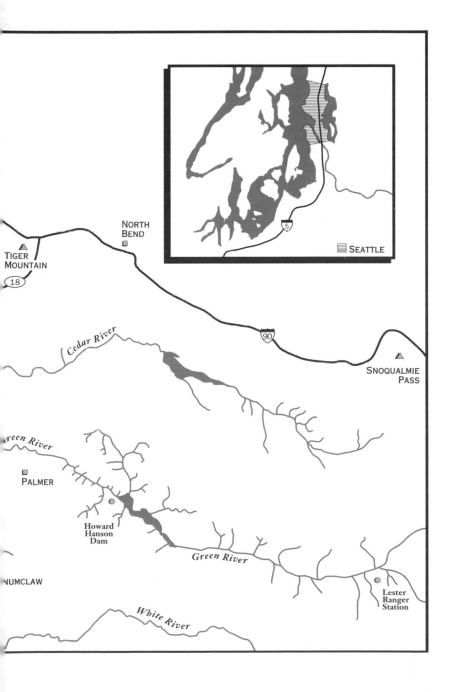

NORTH BEND

TIGER MOUNTAIN

18

Cedar River

90

SNOQUALMIE PASS

Green River

PALMER

Howard Hanson Dam

Green River

NUMCLAW

Lester Ranger Station

White River

SEATTLE

5

Foreword

As a 17-year-old kid from Los Angeles, my first view of the Green River Valley looked like something out of another time. It was 1958 as my plane made its approach to Sea-Tac over a verdant valley whose textured fields spread out in every direction. Farmers moved across the land. And where the earth had recently been turned, great flocks of gulls and waterfowl were flecks of bright white against the stark nakedness of the soil.

Over the next decade, the easy drive from the city would bring me again and again to this place where I followed the wintering birds in one season and savored the smell of the fresh tilled land or the cut produce in another. My friends and I would range far and wide in this easy open land to fly our hawks and falcons and then pack home more berries and vegetables than we could ever expect to eat. Just being in this place gave one the feeling that it was composed to nurture life.

In the more than thirty years that have passed since those romantic 1960s, the face of the valley has been tragically disfigured and its unique cornucopia relationship to Seattle lost forever. To be sure, there was a period when people stood their ground and won a few reprieves for the region, but gradually and overwhelmingly the mindless tide of "highest and best use" swept an unsightly collection of warehouses, asphalt, and malls across the valley floor.

Mike Sato's book pieces together the historical puzzle that is the Green River Valley. From prehistoric to contemporary, and from geologic to political, we learn of the events and forces that shaped this remarkable place in Washington. It is from such chronicles that wisdom is fashioned. While some of the conditions of the valley were determined by nature, others were shaped by the choices of people. Mike Sato's account provides us with the resources to make better choices when it comes to deciding the future of the few valleys that remain to be stewarded for nurturing life.

Tony Angell

Acknowledgments

The voices that are heard in this small book come from many people, some of whom are not identified in its pages.

For generously sharing their time, knowledge and opinions, my thanks go to Tony Angell, Holly Coccoli, Tom Exton, Charlie Fullmer, Steve Haecock, Judith Herring, Joe Henry, Paul Hickey, Grant Jones, Ilze Jones, Ted and Jean Mallory, Bob Matsuda, Curt Miller, Lyle Price, James Rasmussen, Pat Sumption, Trudy Thomas, and Bob Tidball.

For their help in research and photos, I am especially in debt to Howard Fox of the Seattle Public Library, Patricia Cosgrove of the White River Valley Historical Museum, and Stan Greene of the Renton Historical Museum.

To Kathy Fletcher, Deborah Taylor, and my colleagues at People, For Puget Sound, thank you for your patience, good-humored support and for not letting me forget I was supposed to be writing a book.

To David Sato, who was told many times too often that I was too busy writing a book to play with him, thank you for trying to read the first draft and saying honestly: "This is OK if you are really interested, otherwise you would put it down and watch TV."

And to John Beal, to whom this book is dedicated, thank you for being the person you are.

Introduction

A STORY TO BE TOLD

THE DUWAMISH RIVER passes under the shadow of the low-arched West Seattle Bridge and quietly empties into the south end of Seattle's Elliott Bay. The river's greenish-brown waters are neatly defined in its short and narrow valley by fortified banks along which container ships dock, cargo is warehoused, and plants and factories clank and hum.

The waters of the Duwamish come from the rain- and snow-fed Green River, which rises at the crest of the Cascade Mountains 73 miles from Elliott Bay, plunges through a carbonaceous canyon it has gouged, and is fed by foothill streams, before slowing and entering its broad, flat valley plain. The Green River's boundaries are also easy to trace if you follow its serpentine meander along the valley floor, past levees that protect the few farms remaining among the warehouses, office buildings, and shopping centers. Where the valleys of the two waterways meet, the Green River quietly becomes the Duwamish River.

These rivers were not always quiet waters. The floodwaters of the rivers created and, until recently, periodically rejuvenated the valleys. The Duwamish Indians, the first people to settle this land, lived by the seasons and cycles of the rivers, its fish and its floods, its bounty and its hardships. Immigrants later farmed the fertile valleys and fished the estuary, main stems, and tributaries. The rivers determined what did or did not happen on the land.

But 91 years ago, a great flood swept down the river valleys. Out of that flood arose a determination among civic leaders to bring the rivers under their control. The guiding vision was to tame the rivers by dredging their channels, leveeing and diking their banks, and controlling their flow. The land in the valleys was too valuable to be left sitting under water.

Since the great flood of 1906, dredging and rechanneling the Duwamish River has made Elliott Bay one of the busiest ports on the West Coast. Damming the Green River provides Tacoma's drinking water and controls winter floods. Manipulating the amount of water that

flows down the flood plain of the rivers has made the fertile valley land too expensive to farm; civilization's advance of industry, asphalt, and concrete grows in place of pastures, vegetable fields, and berry patches.

The West Seattle Bridges, new and old, span the mouth of the Duwamish waterway. (photo by Ken Lans)

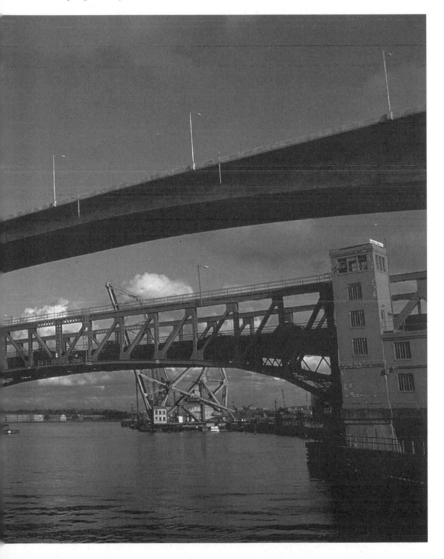

Taming the Duwamish and Green Rivers has brought progress and profit, but the price paid is a daily life cut off from the waters that once nurtured the land and its people. As artist and naturalist Tony Angell asks, "At what point does a river become a sewage canal?" By cutting the trees, clearing the banks, filling the wetlands, dredging the shallows, and flushing our wastes into the river's waters, we have made the migratory highway of the mighty salmon the repository for our pollution.

"When I was a little boy," writes Seattle native Doug Brown, "our closest family friend took us swimming in the Green River. That still forms my images of what a river should look like, the vegetation along the banks, the sand bars and gravel banks, the small fish that played around your legs . . . all enveloped in the dry, soft Northwest summer sunshine." If, as we drive through the modern sprawl of the Puget Sound area, we feel an emptiness of something lost in all that we have gained, it is because, as residents of this land, we too are the people of the Duwamish and Green Rivers. We find ourselves cut off from the salmon and shellfish and birds and wildlife with whom we once shared the seasons of the waters.

Those who dammed and dredged the rivers, hardened their banks, and poured concrete and asphalt over the land are people of the Duwamish and Green Rivers, too. It is their vision that has prevailed. But there are people today who see the river valleys as places worthy of protection and restoration. This community, still small but slowly growing, is found along the banks of the rivers and tributary streams, in their valleys, and on their hills. It is a community that cares for places along the rivers and the natural systems that connect the land and the water. It is a community that seeks to give back to the rivers a small measure of all that has been taken from them.

Compared to how dams, dikes, and dredges dramatically changed the rivers and their people, the efforts of the new river stewards are small and scattered. Much of the land and its waters in the Duwamish and Green River Valleys are still seen by eyes focused on progress and profit. But there is another story of how, in small places, the rivers and their valleys are seen in ways that speak to what our future as their stewards can be.

Chapter One

THE DUWAMISH AND
GREEN RIVER WATERSHEDS

J AMES RASMUSSEN, forty years old, a jazz musician and a Duwamish tribal council member, has climbed to the top of a hill overlooking the Duwamish River Valley in south Seattle. The river here flows brownish green as a backyard to modest riverfront homes in Allentown. The midmorning haze obscures all but a faint outline of Mount Rainier to the south. To the north, there is a peek of the blue of Puget Sound. The steady roar of freight trucks below and jets above is punctuated by gunshots from the Seattle Police Firing Range. To the east, the eight-lane interstate flows like the Duwamish River in its man-made channel. To join James on the hill, you'd get off the freeway at the Boeing Access Road, Museum of Flight Exit 158.

James' tribe, the Duwamish, were settled in the valley well before Captain James Cook explored Elliott Bay in 1792. The hill he stands on is old. The clay and compressed rock is older than the river below and the estuary it drains into, older than the West Seattle hills, older than the mountain in the haze to the south. The hill is the western edge of sediments compressed into rock over 20 million years ago and exposed in the uplifting of the continental plate. Glaciers of the past 2 million years that scoured the Puget Sound Basin have done their work to wear away the hill down to the river plain and to the Sound. Directly below the hilltop's few madronas, firs, and Scot's broom, the ground has more recently been cleared and leveled by bulldozers.

The Duwamish Tribe has been fighting for many years to be recognized by the federal government as a separate and distinct tribe. The fight has been frustrating, but when James talks about the Duwamish—

The People of the River, the Duwamish, along the Green River (photo circa 1900, courtesy of the White River Valley Historical Museum and Society)

the tribe, the river, and the valley—he speaks quietly. "This is a major defensive position for the tribe," James says, using the present tense. He points north to where the Duwamish River empties into Elliott Bay and then up the river to where the mountain's outline looms over the Green River Valley. "When raiding parties would come from the north, we'd pull back down the valley and this is one of the first of several positions."

A British Airways Boeing 737, landing gear down, skims the hilltop on its approach to the King County Airport.

"One of the things this reminds me of is the olden times," James says more loudly. "Especially when you drive down this way and see all the old houses on the original river. Even though things change, this is original river here."

A red-tailed hawk dives and chases a young eagle, dives and chases it again.

James and the Seattle metropolitan area have grown up since the olden times. The days of living by the rhythms of the waters, the land, and the seasons are gone for most people. The many newcomers who have come to enjoy the area's prosperity blissfully see the mountains, rivers, and estuary as unchanging. But the longer you have been here, the more the past, the present, and the future are juxtaposed in what you see and hear.

"The last time I went to Washington, D.C., two years ago, I came back real late on the airplane," James says, quietly again. "I remember thinking, if the old chief was with us, flying in, he would be absolutely amazed not only at all the things that are happening but that it's happening here and that this part of the world draws people even now when we are no longer hunters and gatherers. Some people might say, how tragic. But in a lot of ways, it's not tragic. All of us are still in the middle of a rich area where things change. The old teaching says, it is the place that is important."

Go far enough back in time and this place—these rivers, these valleys, this estuary—did not exist. Not until the Okanogan terrane, island land masses riding on the oceanic plate, "docked" with the bedrock of the Idaho batholith 100 million years ago and, followed by the North Cascades terrane 40 million years later, brought the shoreline of the broad, flat plain westward. The Eocene marine waters lapped at the shoreline at Bellingham, around North Bend where small volcanoes held forth near Issaquah and Renton, down along Enumclaw, and southward through Hood River in Oregon.

Fifty million years ago, the Idaho mountains were drained by streams and rivers that flowed westward across a wide, flat delta much like the Mississippi Delta. Like the Mississippi drainage, the streams and rivers would be carrying and depositing tons upon tons of sediment, building up the delta, and pushing the shoreline westward into the Pacific.

And it would be warm, warmer and more humid than New Orleans on a summer day. Lava and ash from small volcanoes mixed with the delta sand, silt, and clay. The dinosaurs had come and gone, and the time in the sun was for the warm-blooded. For 10 million years, ancestors of palm trees and conifers grew tall, fell, sank, and were buried in the swamps and lakes of the delta plain and covered over by thousands of feet of river sediments.

The continent was on the move. Thirty-six million years ago, the western edge of the continent was being lifted up as it slipped over the Pacific oceanic plate. Forces deep along the contact points torqued and folded and faulted the mile-thick delta sediments and compressed swamp peat. Pushed upward, early Cascade volcanoes divided the delta plain from north to south, built themselves up with lava flows, and wore themselves down with rivers filled with more silt and sand flowing westward. The vast delta plain would now be forever divided into east and west.

To the west, the last of the island land masses rode the oceanic plate and drove into the continent as the Olympic Mountains. The continent was complete at its western edge as the weather turned cooler and dryer and conifer forests took root. The rains fell on the western side of the Cascade divide, and its rivers built the land out to the Pacific.

The continent continued to slip over the oceanic plate. About 25 million years ago, the mountains were again lifted and this time twisted and folded until their rivers ran northwest to the sea. The delta sediments of compressed Eocene swamps were becoming sandstone, oil, and coal as they were folded, lifted up, and covered over by new delta sediments.

The Cascade Mountains as we know them today were fueled from below by the collision of the continental plates. Until about 6 million years ago, they formed a line of fire up and down the coast. The edges of the oceanic plate continued ramming under the continent's delta plain, wrinkling the continent's edge and pushing it upward. Molten rock pushed long fingers up through the sandstones and shales and, where it broke through, spewed forth its lava and ash. It pushed up through Mount Rainier. The foothills were filled with lava, and the delta plain, which stretched to the Pacific Ocean, was covered with ash.

When volcanic activity slowed down, the Cascades were steeper and captured more rainfall; geologists reckon that the ancient rivers flowed northwesterly in the mountain valleys. The ancient Green River sped from its headwaters down the present run of the Cedar River, and the ancient Cedar ran along the course of the Snoqualmie River across the flat delta plain to the sea.

Where James stands looking west over the Duwamish River is about 20 million years older than where the river enters Puget Sound. So are the rocks found further north at low tide at Alki Point, the rocks found at the south tip of Seward Park, and the rocks the interstate cuts through overlooking King County Airport's Boeing Field. These rocks are found at low tide on Bainbridge Island; they are compressed delta sediments formed beyond the early shoreline and lifted up as the continent rose. They are not as old as the outcroppings found near Tukwila and Renton. How this mix of ancient rock defined the land and the ancient waters is hard to tell today from the few outcropppings in the vicinity, because in the time of glaciers, rock is just rock.

Give glaciers 2 million years and they will scour, gouge, and polish the work of 50 million years of sedimentation, fire, and continental collisions. The retreat of each of the four separate glaciations called the Puget Lobe revealed a landscape transformed into massive remains of glacial deposits covering the lowland plains and the Cascade foothills, rock outcroppings polished over, lakes gouged deep, and rivers fed by mountain streams and glacial melt cutting new channels to the sea.

Each successive advance brought delta sands and rocks from as far north as British Columbia. In places, the ice stood over half a mile thick, pushing the mountain streams to flow south and find their way to the sea around the ice's southern edge. After each successive retreat, the sea level rose with the melting ice and the land rebounded from the weight of the retreating ice. The delta plain was rearranged, its low points filled with water, sands, and gravels.

When the last of the ice of the Vashon Glacier began its retreat 18,000 years ago, the lower Green River Valley became a vast lake dammed on the north by the glacier and fed by the waters from the Green and Cedar Rivers as they resumed their northwesterly flows to the sea. The White River continued its flow to the south. The Green River was blocked from its former northwesterly channel and began its flow westward, cutting down through the folded foothills of Eocene sandstone to find its way to the sea. The Green and the Cedar Rivers carried newly deposited sands and rock down from glacial remains blanketing the foothills and dropped them as they flowed into the new inland lake. As the ice finally retreated 10,000 years ago, the inland lake of the Green River Valley filled the Duwamish Valley and joined the new inland sea the glaciers had created. The Cedar River deposited enough glacial material at its mouth near Renton to give form to Lake Washington.

When James' early ancestors began settling the Puget Sound Basin in the wake of the ice's retreat, the climate was maritime, wet, and mild, with conifers reforesting the slopes of the foothills. Standing where James now has to raise his voice to be heard above the incoming jet airplanes, they would have looked down on an inlet of Puget Sound that filled the valley and extended south into the Green River Valley. The inlet would have to be crossed on a bridge higher than what now stands where the interstate crosses over Tukwila; landing at Sea-Tac International Airport would have meant landing on an island. The Cedar River would have dammed off the southern end of Lake Washington from the inland sea and formed a new Black River channel to carry its waters and that of the lake to the inland sea. At Auburn's SuperMall, the Green River was building its delta as it flowed into the inland sea.

The level of the inland sea rose as the glacier melted northward. The land rose from under the weight of the glacier, growing with the silt, sand, and rock deposited by the rivers. Five thousand years ago, Mount Rainier put the finishing touches on the river valley when 2,000 feet of the mountaintop collapsed down the Emmons Glacier into a landslide of watery rock and clay that buried everything from Enumclaw to Auburn under the Osceola mudflow. The mudflow swept down the White River's channel and forced the river northward into the lower Green River Valley. The White River filled the inland sea with the mudflow of volcanic and glacial debris, driving the inland sea back down the valley with each succeeding deposit on its growing river delta.

By the time James' immediate ancestors settled 1,400 years ago on the western banks of the Duwamish River near its mouth, the good rains that swelled the mountain rivers and streams on their return to the inland sea had shaped the river valley by sweeping glacial silt, gravel, and boulders down from the drift plain of the foothills. The heavily timbered slopes along the riverbanks eroded, uprooting entire trees and sending roots, trunks, and branches in rafts of driftwood downstream. Wherever stopped, the river channels overflowed their banks and excavated new channels to continue downstream. The lower valleys filled with the boulders, gravel, driftwood, and silt from the overflows.

The lowland flood plain yielded easily to the waters. River channels were blocked by debris, recut, rearranged, and recut again and again, each time leaving deposits of gravel, sand, and silt. Sediments carried downstream built up the valley floor to over 100 feet in places and, as the valley floor rose with successive deposits of silt and sediment over 10,000 years, the river in the flood plain slowed and meandered. It overflowed during floods, building up its banks with heavier sediment quicker than the land away from the river. Overflowing, the river would split into a main channel and two wider channels on either side of the banks, sometimes braiding and looping back on itself. When the river level fell back within its banks, the land remained flooded.

The faces of the flood plain and the river shifted often in the narrow valley plain below the place where James is standing. Up to here and for about a mile upstream to where the valley widens, the inland sea extended its tides into the river. At the edge of the swamps and wetlands, black-tailed deer and black bears crashed through the understory of sitka spruce, willow, red alder, black cottonwood, wild roses, spirea, and blackberry. On the highest spring tides and when the river flooded, the land belonged to the river and the inland sea. Drawing closer to the bay, the river and the Sound mingled among the bullrush and sedges of tidal marshes. Reaching the bay with its load of sediments, silt, and nutrients, the river built its delta of shallows and tideflats.

The river valley and the tideflats of the Duwamish were fed by the streams that flowed into Lake Sammamish and Lake Washington; the waters of the Black, Cedar, and Green Rivers; and the waters melting off the Emmons Glacier. When the tide was out, the table was set with blue mussels, butter clams, basket cockles, bent nose clams, limpets, horse clams, native oysters, whelps, barnacles, and crabs. On the ebb tide, vast flocks of shorebirds fed on the flats and wheeled in the winter sky. In and around the tideflat's eelgrass beds and the tidal swamps and marshes, fish and waterfowl flourished.

With each season the salmon returned to the river, and with each season the salmon returned to the sea. Drawn by the flow of waters from which they came, the chinook returned in early summer, entering the tidal estuary and moving up the valley plain to spawn in the streams feeding the upper reaches of the Green and Cedar headwaters and in the streams that fed the north end of Lake Washington. They were followed by the coho, seeking out their native streams in the lower foothills, and then the chum, which returned to spawn in the sloughs and creeks of the lowland river. Pinks returned to the glacial streams of the White River. And in winter, the wild running steelhead—seagoing trout—filled the winding river and the lake.

The waters of the rivers, lakes, and Sound gave definition to the land. For the Duwamish—the tribe, the river, and the valley—the time of hunting and gathering had begun.

Chapter Two

THE FLOOD OF NOVEMBER 1906

NINETY-ONE YEARS AGO, unseasonably warm southwesterly winds brought heavy rains to Northwest Washington in November. For the first two weeks, over six inches fell in the hills and high mountains between Mount Rainier and Seattle. The Chinook winds gusted to 40 miles per hour, and snow that had fallen in late October melted in the mountains under temperatures reaching the high 50s.

By dusk on November 13, 1906, the barometer had dropped nearly half an inch, bringing 35-mile-an-hour winds and two and a half inches of rain in 24 hours.

"We have had heavier rainfall in a 12-day period during November," remarked U.S. Weather Observer G.N. Salisbury after the rivers began to flood, "but never so heavy at this particular period."

"The velocity of the wind has much to do with the rapidity with which snow can be melted," said Salisbury. "This month has seen 40 percent more wind than normal. The temperature of 57 degrees is almost unprecedented for this time of year. All the conditions this month have been conducive of excessively high water."

And excessively high water it was.

The Green River's headwaters are in the Snoqualmie National Forest at Green Pass, elevation 4,300 feet, in the morning shade of Blowout Mountain. Waters draining to the east of the pass begin a long journey to the Columbia River and flow into the Pacific Ocean at Astoria. To the west, the journey is shorter: waters flow down the Green River to reach Puget Sound as the Duwamish River.

The Green River at its headwaters is fed by rain, runoff, and snowmelt from Tacoma, Pioneer, Twin Camp, Sawmill, and Sunday Creeks and picks up speed as it drops for 13 miles westward through a narrow gorge of bedrock and boulders. Emerging from the gorge, the river is joined by Newaukum Creek, draining the Enumclaw Plateau, and Big Soos Creek, draining the Black Diamond to Kent Plateau before hitting the valley floor at the city of Auburn. Once in the valley, the river follows a gentle meander northward for 20 miles along a fertile alluvial plain. Reaching the south edge of the city of Seattle, the Green River becomes the Duwamish River, and its waters flow another 12 miles to empty into Elliott Bay and Puget Sound.

Ninety-one years ago, the Green River ran free at its headwaters and Elliott Bay received the drainage from over 1,400 square miles extending north from Mount Rainier to south of Everett. Water from the Cedar River, Lake Sammamish, and Lake Washington watersheds found its way to Puget Sound through the Black River, which flowed into the Green River near Tukwila. To the south, drainage from the northeast slope of Mount Rainier flowed into the White River, which joined forces with the Green River at Auburn, and flowed north to Puget Sound.

The prevailing southwest winds bring clouds that drop 75 percent of the area's yearly precipitation from October through April, most of it in the form of snow at the higher reaches of the Cascades. Near the Green River's headwaters at Lester, snowfall averages about 80 inches and at the higher elevations has topped 500 inches, compared to the lowland average of about 7 inches a year. In the valley, about 30 inches of rain falls in a year.

The combination of heavy rains and melting snow swells the rivers that flow to the valley floor. From each square mile of the watershed, about 40 cubic feet per second of river water flows. At flood, 7,000 cubic feet per second of water rushes down the Cedar River, much of it absorbed and stored by Lake Washington. But the Cedar River's flood strength is paltry compared to the 15,000 cubic feet per second of water rushing down the Green River before it reaches Auburn, and the White River's rate of 20,000 cubic feet per second.

The valley floor from Kent north to where the river valley narrows before reaching Puget Sound is the lowest point of the drainage basin. On that November day in 1906, waters rising from north of Mount Rainier to south of Everett rushed to widen the river at the lowest point on the valley floor to a two-mile wide torrent 24 feet deep in places.

The water cut off transportation along the Interurban rail line that ran south from Seattle and Renton to Auburn. Telegraph lines were downed. Logs and driftwood rammed into bridges, threatening to sweep them away. They jammed at the dike built at Neely's Cut northwest of

Kent, and when they were dynamited, the mass swirled downstream with a roar.

"All houses in the valley at Riverton, Garden Station, Foster, Renton Junction, Orillia, O'Brien, and Kent are surrounded by water," observed reporter Robert Kelsey in the *Seattle Post-Intelligencer*. People fled to higher ground; cows were left stranded on little islands in the middle of the rising waters.

"The valley has lost all aspect of one of the richest farming districts in the state and is as a huge river, with two narrow threads through the waste of waters, the Northern Pacific and Interurban railway lines," he mourned.

The 1906 flood waters brought a massive log jam to the O'Brien Bridge. (photo courtesy of the White River Valley Historical Museum and Society)

The Burke Store and Belgian Saloon at O'Brien during the 1906 flood (photo courtesy of the White River Valley Historical Museum and Society)

Two miles south of Kent, the small town of Thomas disappeared completely under water.

By midnight, the rain was falling even harder.

"The flood was too unexpected to give us a chance to take precautions," explained Board of County Commissioners Chairman Charles Baker. "It is now impossible to do anything in the present condition of the valley."

The river overflowed at Auburn and turned Main Street into a small river. Low-lying homes like the Hemphills' house on the north side of town were flooded and Indian Mary's house was swept away. But Auburn was relatively undamaged, and farmers from the upper valley to the east began arriving in town seeking safety. Parts of the upper valley were more than 10 feet under water, and the raging floodwaters swept heavy log booms and driftwood downstream, destroying bridges, and cutting off roads. At Bloomquist Logging Camp, two loggers drowned while working to save a raft of logs.

Auburn was safe for now, but a mile and a half upstream from where the White River joined forces with the Green River, 3 million board feet of logs and driftwood had formed a barrier blocking the north main channel of the White. As the White River's rush of water and debris slammed into the drift jam, it began overflowing and spreading out, spilling into its south channel, the Stuck River.

When the White River was flowing in its main channel, it wound around the high gravel bluff formed by the Osceola mudflow that marked the western edge of the Muckleshoot Indian Reservation. The White split into two channels flowing north along the Interurban rail line through Auburn and then became one channel again near the cemetery and joined the Green River at 15th Street. When overflowing south into the Stuck River, the White River's waters continued south to empty into the Puyallup River and onto the tideflats of Tacoma's Commencement Bay.

Which way the White River flowed had been an old argument among neighbors. For 20 years, King County and Pierce County settlers, sometimes armed with shotguns and dynamite, had changed the channels of the White River back and forth to reduce their flood damage at the expense of the other. Pierce County farmers had accused King County of dynamiting the gravel bluff on the Muckleshoot Indian Reservation and changing the course of the river southward with a massive landslide.

King County in 1900 had attempted to make the flow of the White River into the Puyallup River drainage permanent by erecting an embankment barrier; Pierce County sued and won an injunction against King County. Later, some King County farmers extended an olive branch to their neighbors to the south and proposed equally dividing the flow of the White River north and south.

King County, however, on that November day in 1906, got rid of the White River for good. Seeking a new channel around the drift jam, the White River cut through the narrow strip of land separating it from the Stuck River and threw its 20,000 cubic feet per second flood flow down the Stuck River Valley into the Puyallup River, flooding the valley to Tacoma with a force of 33,600 cubic feet per second.

The Puyallup River was clocked at flowing 12 miles per hour, overflowing its banks and flooding its lower valley and the city of Tacoma under 6 feet of water. It carried driftwood, lumber, parts of houses, and household furniture out into Commencement Bay.

As the floodwaters receded by year's end, about 300 property owners and interested parties in the valleys turned out for a flood meeting to discuss various plans for the control of the river, "all without acrimony or hard words," reported the *Auburn Argus*. The group established a flood committee and commissioned Major Hiram Chittenden, U.S. Army Corps of Engineers, to study the flood problem and outline remedies.

The following May, the major made his report. First of all, the White River belonged to King County. There were 20 million cubic yards more river deposits on the river's northern flood plain than on its southern course. The Stuck River Valley was a low, swampy basin with no evidence of alluvial deposits from the White River, nor was there any evidence of a well-defined channel in the basin from the White River. There had been "a good deal of interference by citizens of both counties with natural conditions" of the river's course, leading to a major erosion in 1898 of a high bluff on its north bank which slid into the river and shifted its course south. The river regained its former course northward "from natural and artificial causes" until the flood of 1906.

"Whether this last change would, if left alone, be permanent, is idle to speculate," the major said. "But the change itself is a most complete one and not a drop of water now flows down the old White channel."

For the major, the White River, although naturally flowing to the Duwamish, was best left permanently flowing to Tacoma. The question for him was whether the entire White River should be carried down the Duwamish Valley or down the Puyallup Valley, or be divided so that approximately one-half would flow in each direction.

As an engineer, he saw a simple answer: "The distance to the sea by the Duwamish route is about 40 miles; that by the Puyallup is only 20 miles. The slope by the shorter route is much greater than by the longer and the same quantity of water can be carried in a smaller channel."

According to the major, the flooding caused by waters of the Black River that drained the Lake Washington and Cedar River basins would be eliminated after the Lake Washington locks and ship canal were built and the lake level was lowered. That 580-square mile drainage would be diverted entirely to Lake Washington and the channel of the Black River would be abandoned.

The major recommended levees or dikes as the cheapest and most effective way of keeping the river in the valley where it should be. Build the side slopes twice as wide as tall, plant them with a strong turflike Bermuda grass, and keep the banks bare. "All drift heaps and dense willow or other growth should be removed from the channel as to leave it free and open," he advised.

Establish a system of policing the river, he recommended, and every summer burn up drift heaps, cut up trees fallen into the river, and blast large stumps so that the debris will flow down the river when the waters rise in the fall and winter.

With the Black and the White Rivers diverted elsewhere, when dikes and levees in the valley were built and when the river channels were kept clear of vegetation and driftwood jams, the Duwamish River in flood stage would have only the 15,300 cubic feet per second flow of the Green River to carry.

In fact, the stretch of river from Auburn to Tukwila would no longer be called the White River but the Green River, and the valley of its meander would be the Green River Valley from Auburn north to the southern edge of Seattle's Duwamish River Valley.

As for the Duwamish, its dredging and rechanneling would begin in a few short years, and the silt from the river once deposited on its delta would move swiftly into the bay.

"The interference of man with these processes is wholly in the line of arresting overflow," the major proclaimed. "When this has been fully accomplished and all the sediment is forced out into tide water, delta extension will be accelerated and land building in the valley will cease altogether."

The Green River proved that the major was wrong. Giving the White River to Tacoma, sending Lake Washington and the Cedar River out through the Chittenden Locks in 1916, and starting the rechanneling of the Duwamish River in 1912 wasn't enough to tame the river. Almost every two years, the Green River, now reduced to draining only a 474-square-mile watershed, flooded the farmland and residences from Auburn and Kent to Orillia, Allentown, and South Park.

The floods of 1917, 1933, and 1946 were especially severe, with the water in 1933 putting Orillia and Renton under almost 10 feet of water. In all, 11,600 acres of valley farmland and 2,200 acres of town and swamp land were flooded, and damage was estimated at $1.75 million for 1933. In 1946, 12,000 acres were flooded at a loss of $1.3 million.

Proposed solutions abounded. By the 1930s, the talk was definitely centered on building a reservoir to hold the winter storm waters of the Green River. Earlier, Seattle engineers had proposed and abandoned digging a canal from Kent to Lake Washington to divert the flow and floods of the Green River. A proposal to divert the winter flow of the Green River to the Cedar River unfortunately would make the Cedar River Valley a floodway. Constructing a two-mile tunnel from Kent to Puget Sound to drain the river and the valley was definitely too expensive. Building up the levees farmers had placed north of Kent around the turn of the century and diking the rest of the valley to handle a flood like that of 1906 would require a channel and right-of-way 700 feet wide and dikes 20 feet high at a cost of $24 million.

The most reasonable solution, then, was a reservoir created by a dam on the river, and its advocate for the next 25 years was Colonel Howard Hanson, King County's chief civil deputy attorney and chairman of the Seattle Chamber of Commerce's Rivers and Harbors Subcommittee.

"Whether it be for a home, a city, or an expanding metropolitan area, there must be a site, a locale, suited to the purpose by nature or made so by man's efforts," wrote Hanson in a 1957 *Pacific Northwest Quarterly* article, "More Land For Industry."

With a dam built and the Duwamish waterway extended to Tukwila, Hanson believed that "Old Man River, from Elliott Bay to Auburn, will be under control and the entire valley available for its highest and best use."

The major's vision and the colonel's perseverance were the driving forces that would tame the river to serve its people. And when it was tamed, the face of its waters, the land of its valleys, and the hearts of its people were changed in a way that the major and the colonel could scarcely have imagined.

Chapter 3

THE SALMON AT HAMM CREEK

JUST SOUTH OF THE West Seattle Freeway down along West Marginal Way Southwest, the bulldozer and bushwhackers are clearing out the blackberries and Scot's broom for a park at the Port of Seattle's Terminal 107 site opposite Kellogg Island.

In the shadow of the bridge half a mile to the north, the port hired archeologists in 1977 to excavate the area before building its Terminal 105 facility. They found a midden, an ancient camp site, with its huge remains of mussel, clam, and oyster shells. They found stone tools and estimated that the site was occupied for 1,400 years and was abandoned about the time white settlers arrived in the area.

Captain George Vancouver, the area's first tourist, found the campsites abandoned when he visited in 1792, but he suspected that its occupants had temporarily fled. The Duwamish may have already abandoned the site when settlers such as Roberta Frye Watt arrived in 1851. She saw the original river and recalled how her canoe "entered the mouth of the Duwamish and ascended the river between age-old firs and cedars which crowded the banks and made the water dark and shadowy."

Today you see too much of the concrete, asphalt, metal fences, and just plain junk that dominate the banks of what is now the Duwamish waterway. You need some other way of seeing the land and the water.

"It's beautiful," James Rassmusen says, looking out toward Kellogg Island. The Duwamish Tribe has used the archeological findings uncovered by the Port of Seattle to establish their historical presence and tribal identity. It's been a long trial for the Duwamish Tribe to be officially recognized by the federal government as a separate and distinct Washington tribe. The Muckleshoot Indians who have reservation land

and co-manage the watershed's fisheries with the state do not support the Duwamish in their recognition fight.

But James today is talking about what he sees for the Port's park: reestablishing the natural flow of Puget Creek down the hillside where Duwamish were once buried and letting the creek flow through the park and into the fresh-water starved river. It would be a place again for salmon, a fitting place to build a tribal longhouse and cultural center.

"This is a very pretty area, very nice, very calming," James says, turning again to Kellogg Island, now a Port wildlife conservation area off limits to people. "This place is for me the one thing that shows how nature can come back. The island keeps getting bigger and bigger from all the soil that comes down. And the trees. In the seventies, there wasn't anything there, and now it's growing like crazy. It gives you faith that if you are able to leave it alone, it will be OK."

Leaving Kellogg Island alone, much less the Duwamish estuary, has proven to be impossible.

In the 50 years since Roberta Frye Watt paddled up the river, about one fifth of the tidal marshes and over half of the wetland swamps were filled in with soil from the hills to create over 800 acres of "usable" land. To the east, new, buildable shorelands extended from the Spokane Street viaduct south to the First Avenue South Bridge, and on the west, South Park was taking shape. Seattle's early waterfront was formed by covering over 300 acres of shallows and flats with dredged materials and fill.

The river, however, still meandered down the narrow valley through its remaining wetland swamps and tidal marshes and, before reaching the tideflats, swept around Kellogg Island, then a quarter-mile wide, 200-acre intertidal marsh and wetlands surrounded by shellfish beds. Gulls colonized its upland prairie and stands of crabapple and willow grew on its river delta soil.

The island was first claimed by John Pike and originally platted in 1870 as Kellogg Tracts, presumably named after King County Auditor S. Kellogg and county notary David Kellogg. In 1891 the island was called Edwards Island on maps, appropriately named for J.W. Edwards, a salmon sports fisherman who fished from his cabin near Duwamish Head. Perhaps it was the same Edwards who raised dairy cattle and built a barn shown on the southern tip of the island in a 1918 photo. Or perhaps it was the Edwards who diked the southern end of the island and claimed its marshes from the estuary's tides. Or maybe it was the Edwards who let Duwamish Indians build two fishing shacks shown at the water's edge in a 1908 U.S. Geological Survey map.

The Duwamish estuary was prime Seattle waterfront land. (photo courtesy of the Green-Duwamish Watershed Alliance)

By 1910 the days of the river's idyllic meander were numbered, when riverside property owners voted to create the Duwamish Commercial Waterway District to dredge and straighten the river. A year later, the state legislature passed the Port District Act and Seattle voters quickly created the Port of Seattle.

During this time, Major Chittenden retired from the U.S. Army Corps of Engineers as a Brigadier General, after having set in motion the design and construction of the canal and locks that would open Lake Washington directly to Puget Sound. His recommendations for sending the White River to Tacoma had also been accepted, and work was under way to improve the Stuck River channel. At the same time, Renton was busy planning to rechannel the Cedar River into Lake Washington. Flood control and improved navigation and the dredging and rechanneling of rivers in the service of man marched in lockstep. The race for commerce was on.

"Duwamish Valley's Doing Things," the *Duwamish Valley News* announced in 1913. "Cheap Factory Sites in Seattle's Manufacturing

Center." The hoopla reflected a note of petulance about how Seattle's daily press had ignored the waterway project in favor of promoting the Lake Washington canal project. "Sea Level Waterway No Locks," the neighborhood newspaper crowed and pointed to the $700,000 spent for right-of-way purchases, the $148,000 spent for building a suction dredge, and the $400,000 spent on excavating the waterway.

Progress on the Duwamish River did not come easily. Forming the waterway district with taxing authority required state legislation. The Lake Washington canal supporters were suspicious that the Duwamish waterway project was a veiled attempt to kill the canal project. Local property owners along the river bitterly fought the rights-of-way condemnations in the courts.

But money lubricated progress. County voters approved a $1.75 million Harbor Bond Issue that allocated $750,000 to the Lake Washington canal, $600,000 to the Duwamish waterway, $50,000 to rechanneling the Cedar River into Lake Washington, and $350,000 for new Seattle waterfront docks. Money united the new tribes of Duwamish waterway people, Lake Washington canal people, and Cedar River rechanneling people.

In less than ten years of dredging and filling, the lower ten miles of the Duwamish River was "rectified" into a waterway four and a half miles long with three "turning basins" along its length. The river was straightened and its banks fortified; it was deepened and connected to the waters

Rectifying the Duwamish (photo courtesy of the Green-Duwamish Watershed Alliance)

of Elliott Bay. The steam shovels, drag lines, and suction dredge obliterated the river delta and estuarine habitat that had taken 10,000 years to build.

Taming the river at its mouth meant broadening it, deepening it, and straightening it into two 750-foot wide channels, 35 feet deep and a mile long. The mix of tidal flat mud, sand, clams, and worms was dumped to form Harbor Island, covering the bullrush and sedges in the tidal marshes in the areas under and south of the West Seattle Bridge. The dredge cut Kellogg Island in two and built up its east half as part of the new east bank of the waterway. The deep channel immediately began eroding what remained of the island to the west.

Shorebirds, gulls, and crows feasted on the shellfish and worms placed before them by the dredge. But ducks and geese migrating on the Pacific flyway no longer found their customary wintering grounds. Riverfront land, once drained and filled, had become valuable. Inland, the wild places of marshes and swamps were fast disappearing as well. Creeks were diverted, piped through culverts, and filled over.

Moorage for oceangoing ships now took the places where juvenile salmon on their way to the sea could pause for the gentle transition from fresh to salt water amidst the bullrush and sedge of the tidal marshes. Salmon on their return home found the tree-crowded banks they had left were now bare and hard, the waters once dark and shadowy now turbid.

The surge of the incoming tide was still felt along the length of the Duwamish River, but its flow was dramatically diminished by the time the waterway was completed in 1917. Brigadier General Chittenden died that year, a year after the locks that bear his name in Ballard opened Lake Washington directly to Puget Sound. Through the locks the fish and waters from the Lake Washington and Cedar River drainages would now flow, taking away over 60 percent of the Green and Duwamish Rivers' flow.

World War I turned Seattle into a ship-building center with the Port of Seattle as its preeminent landlord. The waterfront boomed with warehouses, wharves, and cold-storage facilities. Airplanes were built, cement was made, food was processed, metals were fabricated, and small communities were established along the banks, on hilltops, and on filled-in areas of the valley floor. When World War II began, all the Duwamish River's tidal swamps and wetlands were gone and only 15 percent of the river's original tidal marshes remained. What remained of Kellogg Island was dredged to provide a storage area for logs and served as a convenient dump for dredged materials.

Industries and houses along the Duwamish changed the way the river smelled to the returning chinook, chum, coho, and steelhead. Sewage flowed directly into the river, as did cyanides, chromates, acid pickling liquor, caustic liquids, synthetic resins, formaldehyde compounds, phenols, pentachlorophenols, acetylene sludges, and arsenic compounds from riverside industries.

As early as the mid-1930s, the deepened channel and reduced water flow combined with sewage to reduce the amount of dissolved oxygen in the river during the late summer and early fall. Chinook and chum salmon faced not only a growing alphabet soup of poisonous chemicals in returning to their ancient home but now found it difficult to breathe.

Until the late 1950s, juvenile salmon heading downstream and adults returning home could find respite amidst the tidal marsh where a spring-fed creek flowed freely down from the hills of White Center into the Duwamish at South Park. Today the marsh is gone and the creek bears the name of Dietrich Hamm, who served as one of the first commissioners of the waterway district and agreed to pay a waterway assessment totaling about one-twentieth of the total district assessment. Hamm Creek finds its way from the Park 'n' Ride at the top of the hill through a culvert under Myers Way, cascades down through a restored woodland, enters a culvert to cross under Highway 509, reappears to flow past an abandoned sewage pumping station, enters a culvert to cross under Highway 99, flows in a roadside ditch between the Seattle City Light substation and Delta Marine Industries, drops down into a culvert, and finally reaches the waters of the Duwamish.

In place of the marsh, there's open field built up behind the fortified riverbank. These are fields where the U.S. Army Corps of Engineers used to pour the slurry of silt they dredged to keep the river deep, sucking up sediments laced with toxic chemicals, a lot of which ran off back into the river. Today, an even deadlier mix of chemicals has been flushed and washed into the Duwamish.

The Duwamish River does not meet state water quality standards, a 1996 state Department of Ecology report found. In addition to having problems with fecal coliform, low dissolved oxygen, and pH, its sediments and waters contain heavy metals such as copper, lead, zinc, cadmium, mercury, arsenic, silver, and chromium; chemicals from petroleum products; PCBs from electrical transformers; pesticides; industrial plastic waste; and wood preservative. Bureaucrats and politicians say things are getting better in the river—or at least not getting worse. That should be good news at Hamm Creek.

It's a short walk from where the culvert to the Duwamish River replaces the original mouth of the creek to some of the most contaminated toxic sites in the state, if not the nation. The miracle is that the Hamm Creek salmon today brave the poisonous chemicals downstream to find the creek after 12 years of habitat restoration work by John Beal.

John's a big man, a Vietnam War veteran, who is sometimes so full of the single-minded vision of what it takes to make a place like Hamm Creek healthy that you can feel his hurt were it not for learning that what he's done for the creek he's done with his own hands, mostly unpaid over the years, in spite of bureaucratic obstacles. Then you want to get down next to John and get your hands dirty too, because working with John at Hamm Creek is like going to church.

"See that barrel?" John says, pointing to the roadside ditch where water is flowing. "I started all the aquatic life you see in that stream out of that barrel. I would come in and seed that barrel, every single month. Things grew up out of the barrel, I'd pull them up and plant them on the side of the stream. Every one of these cattails, every one of these sedges, the small watercress, all of that came out of that barrel, and that's the trick to bringing back streams. Consolidate your habitat in one small spot, something that's protected and given root protection, and then it will proliferate. It works, it really, really works. People come down here and say, 'We'll take that barrel out for you,' and I say, 'No you won't, you won't touch that damn barrel.' You notice that 95 percent of the cattails here have lost their seed except for the three or four that are in that barrel? Now they'll spore their seeds, and their offspring are guaranteed life. Because of the root protection, they've got a fertile layer that

At what point does a river become a sewage canal? (photo by Ken Lans)

keeps the root mass together until it's the perfect time to really bloom. I had one of those in Hamm Creek 12 years ago, and it got to a point where it was giving out so much life I had to take it out. If we do this in these little ditches, we can bring these ditches back to habitat without a whole lot of work. Real slick trick, it really works."

It has taken a lot more than simple, slick tricks to bring the creek back as far as it has come, but that's part of the sermon. Hard work—one log, one stone, one frog at a time—is what it takes. For a city creek flowing through one of the most polluted sections of the valley, it takes being a believer in the regenerative powers of nature to haul out years of garbage only to find the soil laced with toxic chemicals and metals; to develop a filtering system using absorbent floats and plants that break down toxic chemicals; to reintroduce to the creek frogs, crawfish, insects, salmon, and trout fry; and to show and tell the story of Hamm Creek to volunteers, bigwigs, and bureaucrats, but especially to kids.

"What's a place without history?" John asks. "Without a sense of place, you join a gang because that gives you a sense of place, a sense of connection with something to defend. We as a society are losing our sense of defense; we're no longer tribal, we're no longer communal. We are no longer in the situation to love and respect the place we're in so that we nurture it. We're here because that's just where we're at. That's not right."

It seems like everybody these days is talking about restoring the estuarine habitat of the Duwamish. The U.S. Fish and Wildlife Service; the National Marine Fisheries Service; King County; the Muckleshoot Tribe; environmental, business, and community groups; and even the Port of Seattle are making plans, doing small projects, and thinking big.

For the Port, the days of when it dumped 60,000 cubic yards of dredged material on Kellogg Island (in 1974) are long gone. Now the talk is of removing the fill and restoring what remains of the 17-acre island because it is the largest contiguous area of intertidal habitat remaining in the Duwamish. The talk is about the shorelands, the tideflats, the intertidal island, and Puget Creek.

Further upstream at the Turning Basin, Deputy Interior Secretary John Garamendi hailed a joint effort that removed marine debris and created an intertidal beach where salmon could rest between salt and fresh waters as a "perfect example of restoration." He also went to church at Hamm Creek and heard John Beal's sermon.

"You don't eat an elephant in one bite," the deputy secretary is reported to have said. "This little project is a nibble, but with enough of these projects, the elephant will be eaten."

Chapter Four

PASTURES, LEVEES, AND TOWNHOUSES

Walk or bike the river levee trail that extends from Southcenter to Kent's Riverfront Golf Course on a warm Sunday afternoon and the path is deserted, the office buildings and acres of parking lots eerily silent, Mount Rainier looming in the south.

Sealth, chief of the Duwamish, would understand the feeling of strangeness the stillness brings. He is supposed to have said, "When the streets of your cities and villages are silent and you think them deserted, they will throng with returning hosts that once filled and still love this beautiful land." He didn't think the settlers understood the Indian's ways. What the white man understood was what was his, what he could do with what was his, and how he could get more and call it his: "One portion of the land is the same to him as the next, for he is a stranger who comes in the night and takes from the land whatever he needs."

Chief Sealth was dead right in recognizing that for the newcomer "the earth is not his brother, but his enemy." But he was dead wrong when he thought that "when he has conquered it, he moves on."

Not in this valley.

The Oregon Donation Act of 1850 offered 160 acres to a single settler and 320 acres to a married couple to homestead western lands. The intrepid were not long in coming. Some came over Naches Pass to Fort Nisqually and Steilacoom, others came from Portland, and others sailed into Alki. Settlers moved up the Duwamish River Valley, settling along the Black River and on the river's broad valley plain. The salmon ran heavy in the fall of 1854, and Indians from throughout the area came to the river to fish and dry their catch alongside where settlers had staked claims.

The following January, when the tribes agreed at Mukilteo in the Treaty of Point Elliot to "hereby cede, relinquish, and convey to the United States all their right, title, and interest in and to the lands and country occupied by them," the river reportedly overflowed and flooded the entire valley. By the time the Indian War broke out later that year, Brannan, Lake, Jones, King, Cox, Beatty, Thomas, Curtland, Russell, and Thompson had claimed land where the river swung west across the valley floor between what was to become Auburn and Kent. Where the river resumed its northward flow along the valley floor to the west, Cooper and Neely staked claims.

The land first claimed was river grass prairie, relatively free of the native cottonwoods, alders, firs, cedars, and willows and the tangled underbrush of salmonberry, wild roses, and nettles. The white settlers staked claims along the river where the first people of the river, the Duwamish Indians, fished for salmon from weirs in the fall and where they spent their winters in cedar longhouses. Their customary places were where the White and Green Rivers converged, at Mill Creek where the river began its meander from east to west across the valley floor, where the logs jammed at O'Brien, and where the Black River flowed into the Green River.

The land was fertile valley soil, three-quarters of which was later classified by the U.S. Department of Agriculture (USDA) as good or excellent. Ten thousand years of overflowing its banks and building the flood plain higher brought deposits of rich, organic sediment along its reach across the valley floor. Of an estimated 80,000 acres of Class I and Class II soils identified by the USDA in the Puget Sound basin, most of this prime agricultural soil was in the Green River Valley.

The Duwamish who fished, hunted, and foraged laid no claim to live on the land when the settlers who fled the killings of the Indian War returned. Thomas, Neely, Russell, and Joseph Brannan returned to their claims; William Brannan and family, Harvey and Eliza Jones, George and Mary King, and Enos Cooper had been killed. Moses Curtland returned to sell his claim to Thomas Alvord, who amassed 1,100 acres to become the father of farming in the valley.

Alvord, according to Green River Valley historian Stan Flewelling, grew a cornucopia of potatoes, onions, wheat, oats, cabbage, turnips, carrots, peas, hay, barley, and rice in the rich valley soil. He started orchards of apples, pears, and plums. He raised horses, cattle, oxen, hogs, and sheep. He brought in an ox-driven threshing machine from around Cape Horn. He built Alvord's Landing at his farm where the river today flows past Kent's wrecking yards, shipped his produce on his own scow down the river to Seattle, brought supplies back upriver, and made Alvord's Landing the hub of commerce for scows and steamboats in the south valley. An early pioneer of valley warehouses, Alvord built storage sheds, barns, and silos. He ran a store out of his home. And, by 1886, he had established one of the first large-scale dairy farms in the valley, keeping his milk cool in cans anchored to floats in the river.

Alvord spared himself the boom and the bust of the hops-growing craze that transformed the valley into one of the richest areas in the country during the last 15 years before the turn of the century. Hops, first sold

A multi-racial threshing crew in the Lower Green River Valley (photo circa 1910, courtesy of the White River Valley Historical Museum and Society)

to beer brewers locally, were shipped across the country and to as far away as England. Lands were cleared and fortunes made. Fetching a dollar a pound while costing only 10 cents a pound to bring to market, hops made farming glamorous.

Indians from around the region harvested most of the hops as day laborers coming by canoe or on foot, later by the Interurban train, and camping out on the farms. By the early 1890s, Japanese and Chinese immigrant laborers brought in the harvest, and the boom continued until the 1893 depression and the hops louse, an aphid, killed the industry. Fortunes were lost, but the land had been cleared.

The valley farmers knew the river's blessings and heartbreak. Notwithstanding the seasonal flooding, they waited for the land to dry out in the spring, pastured where it was too wet to till, and worked around the flood plain's wetlands. They took sides in the dispute over which way the White River should flow. They formed levee districts to keep the river within its banks. Like all farmers, they watched the weather. And when the waters rose, they watched the levees.

A levee is an embankment built to prevent a river from overflowing. Overflowing its banks is the nature of a river, and a levee is also the natural embankment of heavier sediments deposited by the river wherever it overflows. In time, as the slope of a river's banks gets less steep, a river with a strong enough flow, such as the Green and the White Rivers combined, develops sinuous curves on its flood plain. These curves develop when part of a river's bank erodes enough to deflect the current of its flow far enough into the opposite bank and back again. These deflections begin by creating small bends where the water moves faster in the deeper pools on the outside of the bends and where the water moves slower and deposits sediments in the shallows on the inside of the bends. When the bends get prominent, a river gets grand names like Brisco Meander, Nursery Bend, Horseshoe Curve, Horsehead Bend, or River Bend.

To the extent that a river is a dynamic, changing system, the work of man as engineer has been to control and channel that dynamism. Farmers and their levee districts built up the sides of the Green River and straightened out bends. The higher they built the levees, the longer it took for the water that ended up on the opposite side of the embankment to drain from their fields and pastures. By modifying the bends in the river, they risked having the flow of rushing floodwaters increase its scouring of the bank and having the bank collapse.

But flood losses were well offset by the bounty the flood plain soil brought forth, which was sold at the growing markets of city dwellers to the north. At the turn of the century, farmers like Thomas Alvord were selling milk to Seattle, but the real boom came when Carnation and Borden opened processing plants for condensed milk. Like the international market boom in hops, the dairy boom enticed valley farmers to become dairymen, producing for a national market that flourished until the late 1920s.

Japanese farmers leased land in the valley and grew potatoes, some bought land and grew berries, some joined in the dairying boom, and many truck-farmed a wide variety of vegetables for Seattle's markets.

In its 1948 report on flood control in the Green and Duwamish River Valleys, the U.S. Army Corps of Engineers recounts U.S. Department of Agriculture estimates of a total gross farm income from the 17,600 acres in production in the valley as $4 million in 1946. "Despite the frequent flooding, which has always handicapped the agricultural development of the valley, most of the farm units are small and intensively cultivated," the report notes. Dairy products produced $1.4 million, berries and vegetables $1.2 million, and bulbs and poultry over half a million each. A flood-control dam would mean both converting agricultural production to higher-value crops and converting farmlands to industrial sites. The Corps report authoritatively predicted that half of the 17,600 acres of usable valley land would remain in farming and, by producing higher-value crops, a net annual benefit of nearly a quarter of a million dollars would come from flood control.

Now it was only a matter of time before a dam was built by the Corps to take care of the flooding problem once and for all. By the mid-1950s, politicians and planners began smelling the winds of change that developers had been smelling for over a decade.

The 1954 Development Plan for the Duwamish and Lower Green River Basin prepared for the city of Seattle, King County, and the Port of Seattle projected a 1970 population of one million in the Seattle metropolitan area and a need for 4,000 acres of additional industrial land. The Duwamish River Valley could provide 1,500 of those acres; the lower Green River basin to 180th Street South at Orillia could provide the additional 2,500 acres needed. South of that industrial Maginot Line, the land would be agricultural.

The King County Planning Commission in 1957 estimated that 70,000 people would be calling Renton, Kent, and Auburn home by 1970. Of the 58,000 current residents, only 1 percent worked in agriculture and only 300 families farmed full time. The new family of the valley was young, in their thirties, many with two wage earners in skilled, semiskilled, and semiprofessional work. Eight out of ten owned or were buying their homes. Two-thirds commuted, and traffic volumes were expected to grow by a third by 1970.

Auburn blackberry farm and Future Farmers of America (photo circa 1940, courtesy of the White River Valley Historical Museum and Society)

While the Planning Commission recognized that the valley was ripe for future development, it noted that, if land to be proposed zoned for industry were fully used, only 5,740 acres would remain in agricultural production. They were right. By 1980, there were only 6,755 acres of agricultural land remaining in the lower Green River Valley, and even those acres carried a footnote that some had already been approved for conversion but remained in agricultural use. In a short 20 years since the dam was built and the river was tamed, the valley lost more than 9,000 acres of farmland and gained more than 10,000 acres of developed land.

Under this kind of development pressure, the question for Green River Valley farmers was, why farm? Why farm in the valley when property values were rising as a result of flood control and the opening of Interstate 5, 405, and the Valley Freeway? Why farm in the valley when speculators were speculating, property taxes were being assessed on the basis of highest and best use and on the value of comparable properties that had been developed, and assessments were soaring for local sewer, road, and water system improvements?

Why farm? And why farm in the valley?

"Farmlands preservation was a Seattle thing," says retired *Valley Daily News* reporter Lyle Price, whose beat ranged from Olympia politics to the Kent City Council from the late 1970s to the mid-1990s. "The farmers in the upper valley liked it, but there wasn't much interest among the declining ranks of the older farmers in the lower valley. The first time the bond measure went down to defeat, the majority of South County voters didn't vote for it, and when it finally passed, only a bare majority of South County voted for it."

Lyle sits in the air conditioning of Mom's Place in downtown Kent with his jacket on because he is recovering from a summer cold. He's walked down from where he lives on Scenic Hill, an early subdivision developed by farmer Thomas Alvord's son, Irving. When he's not taking his daily walks around Kent and the valley floor, he's often studying Spanish.

At the beginning of the 1950s, Kent's city limits included a little more than one square mile of incorporated area. In 10 years, Kent's city limits tripled, and so did Auburn's. Speculators, it's been said, were the only ones doing long-range planning: buy up farmlands, ask for annexation, and get zoned for industrial and commercial use. Local residents, according to Lyle, often didn't perceive the changes or, if they did, didn't express alarm. More rental apartments were seen as meeting a need for

47

affordable housing by a well-meaning city council; nobody paused to ponder how the balance might be shifting. "How many people who live here were born here?" Lyle asks. "Newcomers don't see the river here because everybody's commuting north and south. There's been little citizen involvement because most of the people who live here are new and 60 percent of them are renters. I wrote a four-part story in the late seventies about the Soos Creek Plateau, which then had a population of about 100,000, and about King County's rezoning, which would allow a density of 300,000. That's a 72-square mile area, about the size of Seattle, and there were no provisions to set aside funding for any major road improvement. Yet community interest was very low. At local community meetings to draw up the Soos Creek Rezone Proposal, King County staff outnumbered citizens by about two and a half to one. At the final meeting of the King County Council when the rezone was passed, there must have been about 300 developers and lawyers there—and a few actual local residents."

Lyle's still a good reporter who just tells the story. "The pink townhouses you refer to where the Kent-Des Moines Highway crosses the river, that's Signature Pointe. That went in in the eighties after the blue ones we called the Barracks (River Park) went in. The land had been zoned commercial for 15 to 20 years and leased as farmland. There was very little protest, just a complaint from a homeowner on the hill overlooking the property who was unhappy about losing her scenic view. No other houses existed—just farmlands."

So, why farm, and why farm in the valley?

"You farm because you need food. In this valley, there's good soil, good climate, and a good market," says Bob Tidball of T&M Berry Farms, a U-pick farm located near the wrecking yards of Alvord's Landing and the old town of Thomas along 78th Avenue South. North of Auburn and south of Kent's city limits, this area is zoned agricultural by King County.

Bob, a retired Boeing engineer, bought his eight acres just about the time when King County voters in 1979 approved, after two unsuccessful trics, a $50 million farmlands preservation bond, which allowed the county to purchase from landowners the development rights to selected farmlands. Bob's 8 acres are among the 1,000 acres in the lower valley under farmlands preservation, as are 900 acres in the upper valley. An additional 100 to 150 acres in the Thomas area not under the farmlands preservation program are supposedly protected by being zoned agricultural, and their development is limited under the county's agricultural district policies.

But in 1996 developers argued that the King County Council should revise its agricultural district policies to allow rezoning a 26-acre parcel and a 20-acre parcel that hasn't been farmed in 30 years. Rezone to industrial. "Industy takes the best land first and that's the farmland," says Bob. "Developers buy in cheap, sit on the land, and then destroy farming."

Building on agricultural farmland not only takes land out of production but also harms adjacent productive land by blocking subsurface drainage and forcing water to accumulate on the remaining farmlands. Unless one is raising blueberries or cranberries, standing water is not good for berry operations.

"Changing the policy means that there will be no protection of agricultural lands except for the handful that are under farmlands preservation," says Bob, today discouraged. "Authorizing that rezone means that all of the 78th Avenue farms will be lost and, eventually, so will the west side of the valley. As each of the older landowners die, their heirs sell their lands because they aren't farmers. The per-square-foot contribution of agriculture to the local economy is just as important as a factory's. But when you lose farmland, you lose it forever."

Why work hard to keep farming in the valley?

"There's a dairy farm every year moving to the other side of the state from here," says Steve Haecock, who has the driving duties on a tour from South Park to Auburn and back to the business park in Tukwila. "Yakima, Ellensburg—that's losing an industry that generates $50 to $60 million a year in King County."

Steve's been with the King County Conservation District for five years after getting a degree in geology and environmental planning. On today's tour, he's the junior member of the team that provides free advice to farmers on best management practices. Joe Henry, who has been with the Conservation District for nearly 30 years, back to when it was called the King County Soil and Water Conservation District, gets to go along for the ride.

The tour of the valley farmlands has been punctuated by Steve and Joe pointing out a few farms under the preservation program: Smith Brothers Dairy, berry fields, Mormon church property south of Segale's, and the racetrack warm-up property south of 212th.

Joe contends that the farmlands program was supposed to be a three-pronged approach, of which purchasing development rights was only one prong. The other two—economic and technical assistance to keep farmers farming in the valley and the streamlining of regulations to allow them a level playing field with other regions of the state—are only now being grappled with by the County Agricultural Commission.

"Remember, you always have to protect what you've already protected," Joe says, riding down the Valley Freeway. "There's a little valley still in King County where there are raspberry farms that someone wants to develop by changing the zoning." He's talking about Bob Tidball. "It went before the County Council and they split right down the middle."

"I think agriculture in the county has more than just an economic angle; it has more of a cultural value," Joe says before getting out of the car in the parking lot back in Tukwila. "It is hard because you can't put a dollar value on being able to take a child from the city of Seattle out to the county farm. You can't put a dollar value on that, and probably you shouldn't even try. We should probably just say as a society that this is important because we know it's important."

Chapter Five

SOUTHCENTER TO SUPERMALL

Some baby boomers remember the days before the first traffic signal in Bellevue; some talk about horseback riding in the pastures where Interstate 5 and 405 meet, although it's hard to remember from the parking lot at Southcenter Mall exactly how the fence lines ran.

Conservationist Harvey Manning calls it "Tukwilazation"—civilization's propensity to transform river valley bottom land into sprawling low-rise office parks, shopping centers, and warehouse industrial parks, and to connect them with asphalt and concrete roads and walkways. Leave some trees and ponds where they won't get in the way, but enough so that they can be called amenities. It's neat and clean, a far cry from the mess of marsh and river floods of 90 years ago.

The land here, once under the inland sea, remains under its influence. The Cedar River dropped enough glacial sediment at the southern end of Lake Washington to define its shores, and the Osceola mudflow and the White River pushed enough sediments down the valley to get the land about 5 feet above sea level and 20 feet above mean low tide.

Until 1916, the Black River emptied Lake Washington from around the Renton Airport, picked up the meandering drainage of the Cedar River north of where Rainier Avenue South and the Valley Freeway transmogrify, looped around the Eocene rock outcroppings north of the Renton Sewage Treatment Plant, joined the Green River at Fort Dent Park, and became the Duwamish River wending its way to the Sound.

At high tide, the flow of the Black River slowed as it reached the Green River, and when the Green and Cedar Rivers ran full with floodwaters, the Black River overflowed its banks, flowing back to Lake Washington, and the land was returned to the waters. In the Chinook jargon

The Black River drained the Lake Washington and Cedar River Basins before the Chittenden Locks were built. (photo courtesy of the Renton Historical Museum and Society)

of the tribes and white traders, this was Mox La Push, the "river of two mouths."

When the settlers arrived, they found the Hwadaomish (the Duwamish), or the people of the Hwadao (the river), living on the Black River. The people of the river lived there 1,400 years ago in a longhouse. (Construction of a Sears and Roebuck store in 1960 at the Renton Shopping Center uncovered the archeological remains of an active trading center). They lived near both mouths of the river and where the stream draining the east hills of the valley flowed. They lived in the shadow of ancient cedars and firs and amidst blackberries, salmonberries and chokecherries. They dug the camus root. They fished for salmon, smelt, whitefish, and chub; they traveled to the Sound to harvest littleneck clams, horseneck clams, and oysters; they hunted with spear and harpoon; and they traded beaver pelts for metal and ornamental beads.

Isaac Ebey in 1849 gave the first written account of the Black River and identified "very fine opportunities for mill privileges" along a few miles of its rapids. In a few years, the forefathers of Renton and Tukwila were operating a sawmill along its banks, mining coal at the feet of Beacon Hill and the east Renton hills, and hailing the mosquito fleet of shallow-draft sternwheel and sidewheel steamers plying the river at high tide to and from Lake Washington and the coal mines around Lake Sammamish.

About 200 Duwamish lived along the river just before tensions with the growing number of white settlers erupted into the Indian War of 1855. They fished from weirs, guided the settlers, and raised potatoes on small plots. Some Duwamish joined the war; the others were relocated to Fort Kitsap on Bainbridge Island. When hostilities abated in a few years, settlers began returning to the river and, although prohibited, so did the Duwamish.

When ordered to leave, they refused and are reported by Indian Agent George Paige as having said: "This land on Black River belongs to us—our Fathers died here. Their bones are buried here; and we also will die here." And to make it clear: "We do not wish to fight the Whites; if they come to drive us from this place we will not resist, but we will lie down and be shot like dogs rather than leave."

No one shot the Duwamish, and no one forced them to leave. They did not own the land but fished the Black River and lived at the margins of the land which, until the Lake Washington locks and canal were completed in 1916, remained largely defined by the waters of the Cedar River and Lake Washington and, on flood tides, the Green River and the inland sea. The waters brought the salmon but impeded progress, especially when in 1911 the Cedar River overflowed its banks and forced the evacuation of Renton. That was enough for the Renton city fathers: the next year they began their own version of river rectification by digging a channel 2,000 feet long and 80 feet wide and moved the mouth of the Cedar River directly into Lake Washington.

Before retiring from the U.S. Army Corps of Engineers, Hiram Chittenden had won his engineering battle to have the locks built of concrete instead of wood and to build two locks instead of one. He had also prevailed in eliminating a lock on the eastern end of the ship canal, thereby assuring that the waters of the lake would flow only to the Sound.

By July 1916, Portage Bay and Lake Union in Seattle were ready to be connected to Lake Washington through the Montlake Canal and connected to Puget Sound through the ship canal and locks. The waters from nearly 700 square miles would find a new level nine feet closer to the sea level of Puget Sound. Water that flowed east from Beacon Hill in the south to the headwaters of Swamp Creek and Penny Creek south of

Building the Chittenden Locks at Ballard (photo courtesy of the Museum of History and Industry, Seattle)

Everett would now flow through the ship canal. Waters from Duvall south to Tiger Mountain, waters that flowed from the headwaters of the Cedar River off of Tinkham Peak and Yakima Pass in the Cascades, and waters that ran through Maple Valley and Renton would now flow through the ship canal. And with those waters went the salmon that followed the waters.

Clarence Dullahaut moved to Renton in 1903 and recalled in 1981 two nice swimming holes on the Black River where the Renton Airport is now and how a lot of kids also swam where Second Avenue is now. "It was a pretty river, meandering along. People used to come up the Duwamish from the Sound up the Black to Lake Washington in launches."

When the level of Lake Washington was lowered, the Black River

The Black River disappeared after the Chittenden Locks lowered the level of Lake Washington. (photo courtesy of the Renton Historical Museum and Society)

became a backwater channel of the Green River. According to Clarence Dullahaut, salmon by the hundreds were trapped in deep pools along the river. Most poignant is the account provided by David Buerge in the words of Duwamish Joseph Moses:

> That was quite a day for the white people at least. The waters just went down, down, until our landing and canoes stood dry and there was no Black River at all. There were pools, of course, and the struggling fish trapped in them. People came from miles around, laughing and hollering and stuffing fish into gunny sacks.

The salmon were gone, but it was great land—if it hadn't been so wet. The Seattle Planning Commission in 1946 rated the area around the Black River as "poorly utilized," with much of the land in brush and unimproved pasture and only a few acres planted in beans. The area is the most valuable available land in the valley for industrial improvement, the report says. "This area needs flood prevention and adequate drainage." Interestingly enough, the land was well suited, despite periodic flooding, for racing horses.

For almost 60 years, horses raced at Longacres until the track closed in 1992. The track was built on the Nelson farm in less than a month, with horse-drawn scrapers, a steam shovel, and men with shovels moving nearly 60,000 cubic yards of valley soil. In early August 1933, the horses were running and with them the dreams of Longacres founder, Joe Gottstein, and millions of race fans. Like crop farming, horse racing was seasonal. They raced in the summer, and it didn't matter that the winter flood of 1946 submerged the track and surrounded the grandstand with a vast lake that spread across the valley floor. It was dry enough to race again next season.

Longacres was built on or near a previous channel the Green River used as it wound along a swampy flood plain down the valley east of its present course and slightly west of the Valley Freeway. Between 1,000 and 200 years ago, a major flood burst through the embankment and the river moved westward across the valley floor in a new channel along its present course. That's not too hard to imagine if one keeps in mind that the difference in elevation between where Longacres was built and five miles south to where the river used to flow is about five feet. Go a little further south to where the horses are running today at Emerald Downs in Auburn and where shoppers seek bargains at SuperMall and the difference in elevation is less than 15 feet. In the Puget Sound region, people call that flat.

Flat it is, and land behind the river's embankments is naturally marshy and swampy. If it dries out in places, it is because the water table of the flood plain drops with the lower flow of the river. With enough time and enough room, water standing on the flood plain will find its own level. Like the river, the water on the east side of the valley floor moves north to lower ground and, following its older channel, still finds its way to the Black River.

The Black River once flowed under the stately cottonwoods north of the Renton Sewage Treatment Plant. Today it is a scuzzy drainage pond where a great blue heron strikes its classic fishing pose. Trudy Thomas and Ted and Jean Mallory, who are with an organization called Friends of the Black, fall silent and are as still as the heron, then explode in exclamations when the heron stabs at its dinner.

"Thirty-seven nests of herons in the cottonwoods last winter," remarks Trudy, a toxicologist at Boeing. "Thirty-nine," offers Ted, a retired Metro civil engineer. "An eagle last spring came and ate some of the young," notes Jean, the granddaughter of Robert Bridge, a Kent farmer and one of the first Port of Seattle commissioners.

Here along the old channel of the river, the city of Renton has 90 acres that the Friends of the Black are working to keep as an urban wildlife preserve. What remains of the river is now "P 1", a flood-control holding pond and pump station built in the mid-1980s to receive the drainage from Springbrook, Mill, and Garrison Creeks and the east valley floor. In the winter and spring, when the Green River is flowing at a flood stage of 13,000 cubic feet per second upstream at Auburn, the pump at P 1 kicks in and 400 cubic feet per second of water is pumped from the holding pond into the Duwamish River downstream. Storm water runoff from the impervious surfaces of the surrounding freeways, roads, roofs, and parking lots drains into the creek to the holding pond. P 1 is part of an elaborate valley system of holding ponds and pumping stations from Auburn to Tukwila to keep drainage under control. When it doesn't rain, however, it's difficult to maintain the site as a wildlife refuge.

"Last summer, there was no water," Trudy says quietly. "The city was working upstream and they lowered the water level by pumping it out so the water wouldn't back up, but it lasted months and months and there was no habitat down here any more. I called and called and called. That's when we formed the Friends of the Black—to show the city that more than one person cared."

The complexities of managing flood control and water quantity, water quality, and healthy habitat are all here at the lowest point of the valley. The waste and the chemicals that end up here in the water come from miles around. And so does the wildlife.

Along with great blue herons, there are coyotes, raccoons, and a couple of deer in and around the cottonwoods, alder, willow, mountain ash, red osier dogwood, Douglas fir, hemlock, and red cedar. There's been a lot of beaver activity in the last couple of years. Beavers build dams, which are frowned upon in drainage areas, so the animals are moved to other areas such as Crystal Mountain and Vashon Island.

Trudy won the battle with the purple loosestrife through a couple of years of hand weeding, but it's going to take a lot more work to keep the blackberry vines back. Ted points out the goldenrod and says the hummingbirds really love the flowering currant. "The little flycatcher would sit on that red cedar," says Ted. They have seen ducks, grebes, cormorants, a green heron, a kingfisher, a spotted sandpiper, and kill-deer at their urban wildlife oasis. It's not scientific, but they feel that outside the refuge there seem to be fewer birds every year.

"The habitat's gone," Ted says. What he means is that it has been taken away.

A weed has been defined as a plant in the wrong place. A flood is water in the wrong place. Then there are plants that live in water on land. That place is called a wetland, and alluvial rivers like the Green and Duwamish and their wetlands are one system of land and water. The land is created by the river and holds the water of the river. Entire ecosystems of plants, animals, birds, and insects have evolved to take advantage of that simple but profound relationship.

A little over 100 years after the Indian War of 1855, developers purchased the land for the Andover Industrial Park and for Southcenter Shopping Mall. The property was annexed by the city of Tukwila, zoned for industrial and commercial development, and in 1961, the first warehouse was built in the industrial park. To build on the valley floor requires breaking the relationship of the land and water. The process is called "preloading" the soil and "dewatering" it by excavating and putting in wells to pump water out of the soil. Then the excavation is filled with six feet of fill to approximate the building's weight, and the fill is compressed and topped off high enough to stand above the level of a 100-year flood. The compressed fill creates an impervious barrier under the concrete slab of the latest "tilt-up" warehouse or low-rise office building.

The rain that falls on roofs, slabs, and parking areas flows and pools to the nearest low point of land. If adjacent property owners develop their land in the same way, the cluster of developed properties stand as

The Longacres racetrack under the waters of the winter flood of 1946 (photo courtesy of the White River Valley Historical Museum and Society)

an island, and water running off the island seeks lower, undeveloped land. At any given time, there is only so much water, and it is only a matter of where it is moved from here to there. That water, at one time allowed to pool, percolate, and evaporate in rhythm with the seasons of the river, today creates its own flooding as storm water, now carrying fecal and chemical pollutants.

Developers complain bitterly about not being allowed to build on land that is wet and called a wetland. In the valley, this kind of construction is difficult but not impossible. Some developers have learned to "farm" wetlands and find loopholes to alter the drainage patterns until they no longer own wetlands. If you start from the premise that horses have to race, shoppers have to shop, and goods have to be warehoused somewhere in the valley, the valley's wetland habitats will be taken away. You can bet on that at the Emerald Downs racetrack.

In the summer of 1996, Emerald Downs opened for horse racing in Auburn. The Citizens Alliance to Protect Our Wetlands had waged a bitter battle to save 17 acres of wetlands included in the 165-acre property on the old White River alluvium that Ron Crockett and Northwest Racing Associates leased from developer Mario Segale. However, the city of Auburn had eagerly approved the new racetrack a year and a half before a decision by the U.S. Army Corps of Engineers to approve the permit to fill the wetlands. A week after the Corps' decision, ground was broken, dug up, filled in, dewatered, and compacted.

"Horse owners, jockeys, and trainers are enthused about the surface," the *Seattle Post-Intelligencer* gushed. "Jockeys are pleased that it shows no tendency to ball up under the hooves of horses or kick up clogs that provide a hazard for jockeys riding behind other horses. 'It's amazing stuff,' said one horseman. 'The jockeys can't believe it.'"

The "amazing stuff" is nearly three feet of fill, very special fill. The bottom 14 inches is coarse sand; a middle 8-inch layer is fine sand; and the top 14 inches is fine White River bottom silt from near Buckley. Bringing the White River back to the valley it used to flood would have astonished Major Chittenden.

The battlefields left to protect the balance of the valley's natural relationship between its land and waters have grown smaller and smaller with the shrinking of the valley's natural habitats. Like efforts under way to restore habitats in the Duwamish and Green Rivers, there's some small hope in new efforts combining drainage management, wetland restoration, and habitat enhancement.

The city of Kent is creating new wetlands to filter and hold the storm water from the development it has previously permitted. As described by activist Lauri Johnsen in a Rainier Audubon Society 1996 newsletter, by 1997 Kent Public Works will complete a combined storm water detention and wetland treatment pond at its old sewage lagoon site south of 212th Street, and a wildlife habitat area on an adjacent 200 acres. The Green River Natural Resources Enhancement Area will hold 300 acre-feet of storm water storage, have space for a native-plant nursery, and eventually have an educational resource center.

"Never in those early days of seemingly endless and intense public hearings to decide the future of the valley floor did we imagine we might still be involved 15 years later," Lauri writes. "In our innocence, we did not know that projects like this don't happen overnight."

Lauri recounts the agonies and struggles with developers, hazardous wastes, funding uncertainties, and countless designs. "But we were not willing to let the city give up on this idea. As city officials came and went, we were there to remind them of their historical commitment to this project."

After the groundbreaking ceremony in the spring of 1996, Lauri and other task force members lingered a while at the site and reflected on the years they'd invested in the project. "We laughed about how our preschool children then were now in college and how unborn children then were now teenagers. We joked about how some of us wondered if we would even live long enough to see this project built. We rejoiced that we had come this far! What a powerful moment in our lives as we realized that we really had made a difference, that we had played a part in preserving something that will outlast our time here and become even more valuable to future generations.

"Projects like this happen when persistent citizens mesh their efforts with equally committed city officials. Can it happen again? You bet!"

Chapter Six

SALMON AS TAME AS THE RIVER

In 1963 Bob Matsuda took the advice of his Oregon State University fisheries advisory and passed up counting fish in Alaska to go to work at Metro as a summer intern, taking water samples from the Duwamish River. He never left and, after 30 years, retired as Special Projects and Research Coordinator and avoided the turmoil of Metro's recent consolidation into King County government.

Back then, water pollution was big news. Signs on Lake Washington announced that beaches were closed to swimming. People struggled to pronounce "eutophication" to show they understood why the algae was growing out of control in the lake, sucking oxygen away from plants and fish. Even though cities were supposedly treating the 6.4 million gallons a day of sewage they poured into the lake, fecal coliform from inadequate treatment and septic systems made the waters unsafe for people, while the phosphates and nitrogen in the sewage were fertilizing the algae. People differed on what needed to be done and how much it would cost, but enough voters finally agreed in 1958 to take one large step forward to work together in treating the region's sewage. Metro, the Municipality of Metropolitan Seattle, was born.

Up until the late 1920s, cities and towns dumped their raw sewage into Lake Washington and the Duwamish and Green Rivers. When that became a problem, they began treating the sewage, and then dumped it into the lake and the rivers. Growth in the region after World War II brought more houses with more toilets to flush. By the late 1940s, State Fisheries was measuring very high fecal coliform counts in the Green River downstream from Kent. Ten years later, the University of Washington and the State Pollution Control Commission found high temperature and low dissolved oxygen conditions dangerous to salmon migrating through the Duwamish River. In addition to sewage dumped in the rivers by Seattle, Kent, and Auburn, industries were flushing over 20 known organic and toxic waste chemicals into the sewage stream. Flushed into the sewage stream or illegally dumped into the rivers, the chemicals ended up in the water.

"We started river sampling for dissolved oxygen, salinity, temperature," Bob recalls. "We didn't have a boat, so we had to use the bridges—Spokane Street Bridge, 16th Avenue South Bridge, Renton Bridge, Orillia Bridge." Routine sampling at the bottom of the river in early August at the 16th Avenue South Bridge, a gateway to South Park, showed less than one part per million dissolved oxygen, a level lethal to migrating salmon. "We began a special study at 16th Avenue South Bridge, and I had to take samples 15 minutes before and after each slack tide. There were two high slacks and two low slacks in every 24-hour period. We tabulated the data on a chart on the wall."

The 16th Avenue South Bridge (photo by Ken Lans)

At the newly constructed Howard Hanson Dam, the U.S. Army Corps of Engineers was controlling the river's flow. "We asked the Corps to release more water and that brought the surface water higher, but there wasn't any rise in the oxygen at the bottom level," says Bob. "In fact, it hit a low of one-half part per million. The Duwamish is a strong, two-layer estuary, with no mixing of the lower salt water and the upper fresh water. The hatchery runs that year were normal, so the thesis was that the fish had detected low oxygen and avoided it."

Early the next year Metro reported that releasing more water didn't make any difference in the bottom oxygen levels at the 16th Avenue South Bridge and that it was the tide that had more to do with oxygen levels than fresh water flow. On the flood tide, oxygen-rich salt water from the Sound enters the river. On the ebb tide, oxygen at the bottom of the water has been depleted by bottom organisms metabolizing the rich organic matter discharged by the sewage plants. When colder salt water flooded the river, the temperature went down and oxygen-depleting metabolism slowed; on the ebb, the water temperature was higher and the metabolism sped up. During the August neap tides, the salt water exchange took twice as long as the exchange during the spring tides, exacerbating the oxygen-depleting metabolism. Since there was adequate dissolved oxygen in the surface layer, the report tentatively concluded that the record run of 30,000 or so chinook that year were either oblivious to the low oxygen conditions or used the surface of the water to pass through.

Maybe releasing more water didn't make much of a difference that August to the chinook, but the Corps had shown it could turn the flow of the river on and off like a spigot—a godlike act for the good of the fish. Somehow the fish have survived, despite all the godlike acts along the river.

If the life cycle of the Pacific salmon and their sea-run trout cousins isn't amazing enough in itself, consider their determination to return as the seasons dictate to a river dammed near its source, dredged at its mouth into a navigational waterway, used as a disposal ditch for sewage and runoff, and leveed, deforested, and dewatered for over half its length.

Under the best of river conditions—clear, clean, cool, and sufficient water; side channels and gravel bars; enough food in the stream—the ratio of fertilized eggs to adults returning to spawn is naturally low but

Overleaf: *Fishing on the Green River (photo circa 1900, courtesy of the White River Valley Historical Museum and Society)*

exact in natural selectivity. In the wild, hardier fish survive, return to spawn, and continue their genetic line.

When naturally occurring droughts dry up side channels, fewer smolts survive in the wild. When naturally occurring floods blow out gravel beds, and collapsing stream banks smother incubating eggs in river silt, fewer fry survive in the wild. When a major ecological change occurs, wild fish populations change, as when pink salmon no longer migrated up the Duwamish and Green Rivers after the White River went south in 1906. It's all in the genes; survival and perpetuation are the rewards of adaptation.

The last-known purely native run returning and spawning in the wild in the river system is the Green River winter steelhead, growing nearly four feet long and weighing up to 36 pounds. These hardy sea-run trout cousins of the salmon travel out to the Pacific and feed on small fish, crustaceans, and squid before returning to the river late in the year, pausing to adjust to the fresh water, and then starting their upstream migration. They return to the sheltered sides of shoals of gravel swept down from the foothill drift plains and find their "beds" in shallow channels under the overhanging branches of riverbank trees. They rise and roll on the surface, dorsal fins spread in display, and spiral and dive to spawn on the gravel. The young steelhead that survive stay in the river and grow for up to two years, then migrate down river, pause to adjust to the salt water before entering the Sound, and begin their ocean journeys.

A salmon-bearing river system in balance has native salmon that spawn in the wild, young salmon that survive the river's vicissitudes and their predators, fish that migrate out to salt water, and fish that survive their journeys to return in sufficient numbers to perpetuate their genetic bloodlines. Different kinds of salmon return to the river at different times of the year. The balance is as complex as the last 10,000 years of the river system's evolution and the salmon's evolution and adaptation to the river system. The people of the river, the Duwamish, adapted to the seasons of the river and its fish. They knew the balance could not be measured in a single season or two of the salmon's return; they knew the salmon would return to the clear and cold snow-melt mountain waters that meandered along the valley floors and emptied into the inland sea.

Changes to the land changed the waters, and both changed the salmon that returned. After 1916, for salmon to spawn in the Cedar River and the tributaries of Lake Washington and Lake Sammamish meant passing through man-made locks and ship canals 10 miles north of the

Black River. The salmon that visitors watch returning behind the glass wall of the fish passage at the locks are not the same as the salmon once native to these rivers and tributaries, but are salmon that have been put back into the rivers and that somehow have learned to return through the fish passage. Only the winter steelhead remains wild in the Green River. A wild river has wild salmon; taming a river requires managing its salmon in a most unnatural manner.

At the Green River State Fish and Wildlife salmon hatchery, early summer is quiet time. Protective netting drapes over large concrete ponds where coho fingerlings looking for a handout wriggle about in water pumped from Big Soos Creek before it levels out and empties into the Green upriver in the upper valley above Auburn.

Salmon hatchery at Soos Creek (photo circa 1900, courtesy of the White River Valley Historical Museum and Society)

The mouth of the creek is at the foot of the ancient Covington Channel where Pleistocene glaciers forced waters of the Cedar River to roar down to the south until the northern valleys were clear of ice. Now traffic roars on the drift plain above the channel on Highway 18 and up and down the channel on the Auburn-Black Diamond Road next to the Quonset hut-roofed hatchery and the fish-filled concrete pools.

The hatchery was established at the turn of the century when the foothill waters of Jenkins, Cranmar, Covington, and Little Soos Creeks ran clear and cold into the Big Soos. The hatchery looked different back then, but so did the area around the creeks above. That was before the Soos Creek Plateau had a name and the name Lake Wilderness meant something.

Charlotte Cormier, a 16-year veteran of the hatchery, says it gets a lot more interesting when the chinook and coho return. They use a large net to collect the fish returning up the creek, put them in holding ponds, and sort them for spawning. Both fish reared and released at the hatchery and fish native to the creek are collected, and there's no way to tell which ones are which since only 5 percent of the hatchery-reared fish are marked by cutting off their antipode fin before being released. Native fish are supposed to be left alone, but the only way to know is to mark all the hatchery fish released so that only hatchery fish are collected when the salmon return.

When the fish are ready to spawn, the females are stripped of their eggs and the eggs are put in buckets. Milt, the fish sperm, is milked from the males into other buckets. Then the eggs and the sperm are mixed in buckets. Somebody comes in a truck and takes the dead salmon and turns them into fertilizer.

Critics of hatchery operations decry the practice of releasing large numbers of fish hatched from the eggs and sperm of too few fish. "We're increasing diversity by taking eggs and sperm from the small fish as well as from the large fish," says Charlotte, who is aware of the criticism. "We're also using smaller buckets when mixing the eggs and sperm and taking smaller samples of sperm to mix with the eggs." The result, she says, is greater diversity, and they are finding higher survival rates with this method.

The hatchery is the largest in the state and supplies fertile eggs to other hatcheries and environmental education programs. In long, water-circulating troughs, the hatchery incubates 12.5 million chinook in deep egg trays and 4.5 million coho in shallow egg trays. To kill fish fungus, a 30 percent formaldehyde solution called formalin is added to the incubation water. Charlotte says that 96 percent of the eggs hatch and in four months the young are moved to the concrete pools where they are fed fish food. Juveniles are released a little after their first birthdays into Big Soos Creek. A lot of coho are supplied by the state hatchery to the Muckleshoot Tribe's Keta Creek hatchery a few miles upstream on the Green River, where the tribe also raises and releases chum salmon. Above the Green River Gorge is the state's steelhead hatchery at Palmer.

There are salmon hatcheries on the river because salmon are a business. Salmon are talked about as a business. The catch is called a "harvest," salmon returning to spawn in certain parts of a river or stream at the same time are distinguished as being distinct "stock," and salmon making more salmon in the wild or in a hatchery is "production." By harvesting an amount of stock based on leaving enough of the stock to produce more stock, you have a "sustainable yield." Just like farming, you save a bag of seeds to plant next year before you grind all your wheat into flour.

Seen as a business, salmon hatcheries make perfect sense. When a native stock's production in the wild falls, hatchery-reared salmon are released to supplement production so that fishermen and sportsmen can catch fish when the fish return.

In 1947 when the Green River was still flooding Longacres and the lower valleys, State Fisheries and Game reported to the U.S. Army Corps of Engineers that building a flood control dam on the Green River would benefit the river's salmon fisheries, which had a combined wholesale and retail value of a little less than a million dollars in 1946. The U.S. Fish and Wildlife Service told the Corps that the coho, steelhead, and trout fisheries in the river would benefit by $56,000 a year by a dam that maintained a continuous flow through the summer.

The Green River salmon and steelhead runs were among the best in Puget Sound. The fisheries had declined dramatically by the late 1930s because commercial harvesting went unrestricted and more and more sewage and industrial wastes were pouring into the waters of the lower reaches of the river. After the state started regulating the harvest and boosting production with hatchery fish, the fisheries recovered, but certain salmon stocks were losing the battle.

By the late 1960s, Interstate 5 and 405 were completed, Metro's sewage interceptor and the Valley Freeway reached Kent and then Auburn, and businesses and housing boomed through the valley and its foothills. Metro's new and expanded Renton Sewage Treatment Plant was treating 24 million gallons a day and now dumping the sewage into

71

Puget Sound. Fecal coliform counts in the river went down and dissolved oxygen levels returned to normal. The Green River hatchery reared and released millions of fish into the river, and there were enough returning to keep fishing. But the native chinook and coho bred with fish produced at the hatchery and the native chum were replaced by hatchery stocks of fish from Hood Canal. Only the wild and native winter steelhead survived.

Throwing more fish into a river system out of balance cannot restore the balance. Because of losing clean water and natural habitat, the native stocks declined, and hatchery-reared salmon, which suffer higher mortality rates than native stocks, cannot supplement the decline. The genetic diversity of hatchery-bred salmon is limited by the relatively small number of fish chosen to provide eggs and sperm; the survival capability of juveniles is limited by their being reared in controlled conditions and being fed until released. The result is fish as tame as the river. Fish folks debate the genetic effect of wild and hatchery salmon interbreeding and new ways of managing release of hatchery stocks. But it is the land and its river that are out of balance, not the salmon.

At the Green River hatchery, Charlotte is much more animated when she shows the pictures of the hatchery during the April 1991 and February 1996 floods when Big Soos sent two and a half feet of water rushing through the hatchery ponds and incubation area. Big Soos brought down silt and mud, and there is more and more silt in the water the hatchery has used for nearly a century. The silt comes from upstream development, says Charlotte. "Fish hatch best in spring water," she says. One plan is to move the hatchery operation to a different location and use the creek only for the growing ponds.

Everywhere people have settled on the glacial drift plain—upstream on the Big Soos and throughout the valley—the salmon's river system has been thrown out of balance.

In an area the size of the city of Seattle Lyle Price talks about, civilization spills over along the Kent-Kangley Road and the county's most recent urban growth boundary gives the west side of the watershed to urban growth; the rest is supposed to remain in densities of one-acre development to three and a half to five acres. The impacts of strip malls, parking lots, and apartments are obvious; those from Christmas trees are not.

"There are seven major tree growers I know of along Big Soos," says John Beal. "In order to get a tree up fast, the growers need to fertilize the living bejeebers out of it. The majority use fish fertilizer, which isn't bad, but they also use manure because you can pile it at the base of the tree and let it leach in. If you look at every one of these tree farms along Big Soos, they all run toward the creek, because if you get the trees too wet, they die, and your fertilizers drain off. During the summer they've got to water these trees, and what they're doing is washing that nutrient back into the stream. Some of the ones upstream have gone to injecting fish fertilizer into the ground, and it's a lot less damaging because it's in the soil and not running off into your creek. Quite a bit more expensive, more labor intensive."

But, says John, you can have Christmas trees and healthy streams. "Plant fewer trees, move away from the creek, and change fertilizing techniques so that everything isn't dumped right into the creek. Build a mini-wetland, a bio-swale, along the length of the creek to hold the water and the nutrients, and reuse it for watering during the summer. But it's less fertilizer and reduction in the number of trees you grow."

But less rather than more is not what the Duwamish Improvement Club or Thomas Alvord or Hiram Chittenden or Howard Hanson saw when they looked at the Green River and its valleys. They saw more ships, more land for industry, more cows, and more houses for more people. Those who followed saw more Christmas trees, more square feet for warehouses and retail stores, more airplanes, more density for housing developments, more milk, more berries, more water, more salmon, and on and on.

The fisheries managers keep pouring fish into the river because it is a sobering time when the nets and lines and boats are out of the water more often than in. But the river has taken a beating and the salmon have taken a beating. Native and hatchery fish both suffer when the river and its tributaries have low dissolved oxygen, high temperatures, and silty, turbid water. They both suffer genetic damage and reduced immunity by having to pass through the toxic soup of chemicals in the sediments, water column, and food chain of the industrialized river. They both live in a river that can be turned on and off like a spigot. They have lost their place in the river.

Chapter Seven

WHERE THE RIVER RUNS FREE

CHARLIE FULLMER is an old-style hard-rock geologist who uses both hands like a pilot describing aerial acrobatics to talk about the plunge of the bedrock hidden beneath the glacial drift plain in the foothills above Auburn.

"That on the bluff up there is glacial outwash," he says, standing next to the river at Flaming Geyser State Park and looking up. "Somewhere below, it's going to Eocene. (His hands start to fly.) See, there are dip components going this way, rolling into the syncline. (The hands move downward.) This is called plunge where it goes off this way. Say you had a loaf of bread. Then you wouldn't have any plunge in it. But suppose you tilted it, then you'd have a plunge. That's also when you might have a structural high."

He looks down to the river. "That's a medial bar," he says. "Very important for fish redds during spawning season. You'd see them in there." Then, back up to the bluff: "Glacial—the flat lines are a giveaway."

For a hard-rock geologist like Charlie, it is often from the little you can see that you figure out what is really going on with what you can't see. He has seen a lot exploring for oil, working out the geology for landing on the moon, mapping King County wetlands, and assessing flood damage. Still, riding over the foothills, looking for the bedrock around the Green River Gorge, he's brought up short by the rapid changes human development has brought.

Further up the gorge, there's at least some permanence in the bedrock in which the river has carved its narrow channel since the retreat of the Vashon Glacier.

"We're looking here at 100 feet of 10,000 feet of this stuff—a microscopic bit," Charlie says, looking down smoothly curved walls of the gorge to the riverbed below. "The lower part is dark carbonaceous sandstone. Not coal, but it has a high percentage of carbon in it."

"This stuff" Charlie refers to is sediments from the Idaho mountains deposited by rivers flowing west for millions and millions of years before the Cascades rose up to divide the delta plain into west and east. This stuff contains the remains of trees and plants that lived and died in the delta swamps, were covered over by tons of sediment, and squeezed into layers of coal and sandstones. This stuff is what the Green River, blocked from its northwesterly channel by glacial moraines and remnants of glacial ice, meandered over and cut into to create a new 12-mile channel in its plunge to the valley below.

It is a magnificent piece of work, a part of the river that still runs free as a result of its singular inaccessibility. The river begins its cut through the Eocene where the state upriver has developed public access at Palmer-Kanasket State Park and leaves the Eocene at Flaming Geyser State Park. Between those points it twists and plunges in canyons 150 to 300 feet deep where the conifers that line the gorge's edge disappear behind sheer and overhanging cliffs.

The coal in this stuff gave names to places like Black Diamond, Carbonado, Cumberland, and Newcastle. Different layers of coal and sandstone, formed at different times beginning about 50 million years ago, were revealed where the river created its gorge. The patterns and directions of the layers gave a glimpse into how the western edge of the continent had been pushed up and down into waves, taking its layers of coal and sandstone laid down flat on the delta plain upward, downward, and sideways with the folds, sometimes cracking and slipping along fault lines under the intense pressures. The tops of the waves have eroded and been covered over by glacial remains, giving little clue to the undulating Eocene layers of coal and sandstone below. The river revealed to the early miners and mining companies where the layers of coal-bearing rock would be nearest the surface.

The river is clear and fast and runs alone without tributaries in the gorge. Steelhead and chinook salmon returning this far are passing through to the further reaches of the upper watershed and find their resting places in the backwater eddies and pools. The river channel is cut where the rock offers least resistance, leaving in places scour lines where parts of the sandstone are softer. On the flat rock surfaces, eddying currents swirling sand around in small depressions hollow out potholes.

Thanks to conservationists led by Wolf Bauer, the river's run through the gorge was designated by the state as the Green River

Gorge Conservation Area in 1968. Out of that designation, the Palmer-Kanasket State Park was developed and the private campground at Flaming Geyser was purchased and developed by the state. The truly adventurous prefer experiencing the river and its rapids by kayak and river raft. In the gorge, recreational boaters get the closest to knowing the free flow of the Green River and the closest to knowing that its flow is fettered by the U.S. Army Corps of Engineers and the amount of water held and released for flood control and fisheries enhancement. The Corps recently made the Washington Recreational River Runners a bit happier by agreeing to take recreational boating into account and to do its best to release water during the weekend when most boaters ride the waters of the gorge. When and how much water is released is up to the weather and the Corps first fulfilling its flood control and fisheries management water requirements. Boaters take some hope that, in wetter years, the Corps' release of a river-running optimum of 1,200 cubic feet per second or more will come in late fall and winter—and on the weekends.

For the less than intrepid, getting more than a view of the gorge from the highway bridges that cross it simply requires a little sense of adventure and ample directions found in trail guidebooks. Developing easier public access to the gorge for picnicking and camping was proposed for several areas along the river's reach; some property was purchased by the state, but it is now held for future development.

But leaving the wild reaches of the gorge to the slightly more adventurous may be just as well for now. The contrast of driving from the rectified tameness of the river's lower valley to where it runs free in one short day's trip may be too much to bear. Conservationists, recreational users, and people who live along the middle reaches of the river see different things when the hubbub of public access at the river's parks reaches a crescendo on summer weekends. Just like Charlie Fullmer's geology, what you can see makes you wonder what's really going on in what you can't see.

At Jones & Jones Landscape Architects, *A River of Green* describes the river from its headwaters to its industrialized mouth but focuses on the river's run from Flaming Geyser to Allentown. Ilze Jones, Curt Miller, and Grant Jones may forget some of the details of the 1979 study they prepared for King County, but the basic concepts remain strong.

"We developed a planning method of segmenting a river into its 'rooms' in the early seventies when we worked on the Nooksack," says Grant. "We were suffering the usual planner hang-ups with information in river miles, feet and inches, gallons per minute, all the kind of stuff nobody understands. The question was how to relate all this to the river. I remember we sat on the bank of the river and it was Ilze who said that looking upstream where the river came from around a bend and looking downstream to where it disappeared around a bend, that this was like a room."

The method from then on was to analyze the river in all of its aspects, define its sections by its physical or historical features, and name the sections of the river.

"Naming places around the river gives people a sense of what the river is," says Grant.

"The key is to link places to people," says Curt.

In *A River of Green*, they divided the river into its reaches: lower valley, upper valley, gorge, and upper basin. Each reach is divided into runs, such as Auburn Narrows, Midway Bluff, River Farms, and Newaukum. Each run is divided into units, such as Park and Lea Hill, Riverpark and Bluffside, Split Channel and Straight, and Whitney Bridge and Two Creeks.

"People have lost the ability to describe the land," says Grant. "Giving the land names along the way restores a sense of place. It gives people a way to talk about the land and waters. It unites them around a place."

"This approach is from the ground up," says Curt. "This is not the usual governmental approach which requires things to be all the same in all communities across the board."

"Planning like this isn't taught in schools," says Grant. "The typical process is not place based. If you are a public entity, your plan is to get the project accepted while only taking into account your own

A riverbank farm in a "room" of the Duwamish River in Tukwila (photo by Ken Lans)

concerns. That's why people on the land don't trust public planners and the consultants who work for them."

The lesson unfortunately was learned the hard way by King County park planners who approached the upper Green River Valley community with a project to develop a trail that paralleled the roadway from Auburn Narrows, the county park near Highway 18, to Flaming Geyser State Park.

Harvey Manning found this valley to be the real Green River Valley and a quick antidote to the development metastasizing on the lower valley floor. Wolf Bauer waxed eloquent about the half-mile-wide valley's "floodway" river braiding between islands of gravel bar beaches and passing stream-side tree groves screening meadows, backwater ponds, and wildlife sanctuaries from human activities.

The river emerging from the Eocene rock of the gorge is joined by several streams and creeks. Newaukum Creek, unfortunately carrying a load of fecal coliform and sometimes low in dissolved oxygen, drains the Enumclaw Plateau and enters the Green River, as does Soos Creek after passing the state salmon hatchery. Fresh, cooler water recharges the river; mainstream gravel bars and tributary streams remain prime spawning habitat for chinook and coho, and the backwater sloughs and ponds are shaded havens for the young.

The valley retains its rural and agricultural feel. The current mix of old-time farms, the horse-lover estates, and those who simply can afford to live there is a far cry from the farmers fleeing to Auburn when the river used to flood. While housing developments close in from all sides of the valley, the land use regulations and farm preservation program help maintain the valley's appearance.

Residents way back in the 1970s had complained about the increasing traffic on the valley road connecting Auburn and Flaming Geyser State Park. Without doubt, the area was popular, and King County's 1989 Open Space Bond provided $2 million for property acquisitions. A trail along the rural farmlands would fit nicely into the county-wide trail system being built.

The community meetings, however, quickly heated up with the objections to the project from angry property owners. Tom Exton, a 25-year county employee who used to oversee both park construction projects and the trails program, had taken on coordinating the county trails program full time a few years before the upper valley meetings. Tom and county officials took the brunt of some residents' fears and anger. At one point, the sheriff had to be called in because of threats to county staff. "A fun time for all," he sardonically recalls.

"No Trail" signs went up along the Green River Valley Road and, by the end of 1992, the King County Council acceded to local resident demands and stopped future spending for the trails project.

"The major objection was that this was an urban development in a rural setting," says Tom. Because the bond authorized purchase of 150-foot-wide trail corridors, property owners got scared.

"We have never acquired 150-foot corridors for trails," says Tom. The residents who spoke up at the meetings accused the county of taking their lands by condemnation, violating their privacy, and opening up the area to more city people.

Any benefits the project might bring to the valley residents were just never listened to at the meetings. According to Tom, the trail would take some bike traffic off the narrow county road and make the roads safer for local residents. The trail would also give local residents quicker bike access to Auburn and to Flaming Geyser State Park.

"The council deauthorized spending for the project, so there are no plans for new acquisitions," says Tom. "Depending on who around here you ask, some staff will say there's no way they're going back. Depending on how things change in the valley, I still feel it will be feasible someday."

More successful in the upper valley were the acquisitions made by the county on the south side of the river to protect riparian habitat and upland watersheds. Among the staunchest supporters of the waterways protection program are former opponents of the trail. The difference, according to Tom, is that the watershed program works with property owners and carries no threat of condemnation.

"If they don't want us to be there, we leave," he says.

The lesson of the upper Green River Valley trail is instructive but perplexing. From what we can see, what's going on in what we can't see? Clearly a community needs to be involved from the very beginning in developing a program or project that will be good for their community. But how is a community to know it will be good for them if they do not already know that?

"Maybe you need to start small," says Curt Miller. "Start with a couple of dynamic places, places like salmon habitat restoration sites, make a trail to those places, then see if you can go farther."

Along the Duwamish and the lower Green River, where there are no communities like the one in the upper Green River Valley, anyone with the same spirit of adventure as explorers of the Green River Gorge can search out some small beginnings of salmon habitat restoration sites.

Hometown River: The Duwamish at its mouth, looking south (photo by Ken Lans)

Start at the new intertidal slough created at Terminal 105, cross the waterway to the reshaped intertidal shoreline at the Federal Way Center, stop at John Beal's Hamm Creek, visit the new sloped intertidal shoreline at the Turning Basin, see Tukwila's streambank restoration at the Southgate Creek Fish Passage, and look for birds at the Tukwila Pond in the heart of Southcenter. While inspired, look for birds and beavers on the Black River at the P 1 pond and at the Kent storm water treatment wetlands.

What's wrong with this picture is that you can't see the whole picture from these few points of light. Not yet. What's right is that these individual projects have been done with the best of intentions to restore the health of the river's habitats. They are pointing in the direction of renewing a balance of the river and the land, a balance of the waters and the people of the land living near the waters. There are only glimmers of the communities that might be built around the "rooms" of these restoration projects. At the Green River Gorge where the river appears to run free, the little you can see still gives the assurance that what you cannot see is wild and free. Sadly, in the valley where the river is tamed, too much of what you can see still makes you feel that the whole river is degraded.

According to the group American Rivers, we should protect our wild rivers and restore our hometown rivers.

"That's your slogan for the Green: Hometown River," offers Ilze Jones. "People live here knowing they live near Puget Sound and Lake Washington, but I'll bet most of them don't know how close they are to having the Green in their backyard." Recreational people, according to Ilze, are the constituents of the River of Green. "It's canoeists, kayakers, joggers, bikers, and walkers. It's no longer the farmers, and it's certainly not the developers. It's never too late. Maybe people have to trash it before they can come to appreciate it enough to want to save it."

Grant Jones dismisses visionary talk. "We don't have a vision that the river has to be a certain way. The river has an intrinsic self. It will always be there whether or not we work towards protecting it this generation. It'll be there if the next generation wants to have a community."

Beginning where the river runs free, there can be small places along the river's reach, small places where restored habitat provides respite for the salmon and birds and wildlife—and the river's people—before the waters flow into the sea. Communities that care about these places will name these places even if the places do not all connect together at first. When other communities restore other small places that provide respite, the names and places will grow. There will be a point when the communities along the river will be able to see along its reach what others were not able to see before. Ultimately, those places and their names will be the river, and there will be many different people of the river.

Chapter Eight

AT THE HEADWATERS

About the same time Water Superintendent William Mulholland was deep in his skullduggery to steal the water of the Owens Valley and pipe it 250 miles to Los Angeles, Tacoma Mayor George Wright filed a claim for Tacoma's fledgling municipal utility to pipe water from the Green River at a more modest 40 or so miles away.

It was August 1906, a few months before the flood that sent the White River permanently to Tacoma, and Mayor Wright, while certainly no Mulholland, was convinced that Tacoma's future could not be left to drinking out of Clover Creek with its ducks, children, and cows or out of Galliher's Gulch with its seeping sewage.

Tacoma was no Los Angeles when it came to water, but when it comes to water, the rules everywhere are hardball. Mayor Wright shut down the city wells to convince the city's voters to approve building the pipeline from the Green River to Tacoma. The voters were unconvinced the first time, but the water situation in the growing town was becoming serious enough for the voters to go with a pipeline.

In 1912, Tacoma finished building a 17-foot-high dam from which it would divert water into its pipeline, and closed off the river's upper 20 miles and half of the river's drainage basin to native chinook and steelhead. It was no big deal compared to opening the pipeline in the middle of summer the next year and having 42 million gallons a day delivered to the city's doorstep.

Locking up a water right of 113 cubic feet per second from a river that was snow-fed and didn't require filtering out glacial silt was equal to the city's rivalry with Seattle; to deliver it to its growing population and water-intensive pulp and paper industries was the kind of progress that would make a city great. But it could only be a beginning.

Tacoma's Headworks Dam, completed in 1912, closed off the upper river and half the river's drainage basin to salmon. (photo courtesy of Tacoma Public Utilities)

Drinking out of the Green River is the last thing one would consider until getting upstream to where the gorge empties out at Flaming Geyser State Park. In the gorge, the water is so wildly spectacular that it would tempt anyone to drink. Still, it is only up near the headwaters, about 60 river miles from the east and west Duwamish waterway, that you get to where deer, elk, black bears, cougars, and bobcats outnumber human inhabitants. The watershed above the diversion dam has been off limits since Tacoma and the Forest Service made an agreement in 1914; the road now has a locked gate at Lester on the east side and a Tacoma watchman on the west side. Ninety-three-year-old Gertrude Murphy is the last resident of Lester, and she comes home only in the summertime. Otherwise, the river is seen only by loggers and truckers, railroad workers, government fish and flood folks, and in more recent years, a few permitted hunters.

If you look at a river as a municipal water supply source, the water is free; delivering it to its users is not. Users aren't paying for the water they use; they are paying for the delivery of the water. If people aren't using water, they aren't paying for building the delivery system. To pay for the delivery system, you want to keep your pipes full and deliver as much water as you can. If the price is right, people will use as much water as they want. The important thing is to get the water and get lots of people to use the water.

Tacoma began replacing its original wooden pipes running from the Green River with steel pipes in 1924 and was taking out 55 million gallons a day by 1942. When it completed rebuilding its first pipeline in 1952, Tacoma was taking 72 million gallons a day from the Green, about 10 million gallons a day less than what its water right allowed. Diverting the equivalent of 113 cubic feet per second in a day down to Tacoma is certainly of a different order of magnitude compared to the 33,000

Main Street, Lester, Washington (photo courtesy of the Green-Duwamish Watershed Alliance)

cubic feet per second of Puyallup and White River waters that roared down to Tacoma in November 1906.

If you look at a river as a vehicle of floodwaters, as Major Chittenden did in 1907, the immediate remedy is to make sure its waters stay as much as possible within its banks by ensuring its flow downstream as quickly and smoothly as possible. Clear the debris, dredge the channels, straighten the bends, and fortify the levees. There was only so much you could do with a river like the Green with relatively little elevation drop once it reached the lower valleys, and a high water flow meeting an incoming tide would overflow the banks. In other words, the Green River flooded because it was a flood plain river.

A reasonable solution, then, was to build a dam above the lower valley that could hold a large enough part of the river's flow during the winter storms and release that water at a rate the river could safely carry within its banks. As early as 1928, local civic leaders such as Howard Hanson were talking about building a dam on the Green River. It was a good idea, even a great idea, if somebody would pay for building it. Damming the Green River did not get serious consideration until after the Great Depression and World War II, when the U.S. Army Corps of Engineers began a formal analysis, and the project didn't get federal funding until a young Warren G. Magnuson demonstrated his prowess, bringing the project home from Washington, D.C.

The dam was no great engineering feat by Western river standards. Since the records of flood flows before 1932 were sketchy, Corps engineers used a "standard project flood" model of a storm like 1906 and calculated how much water needed to be stored in a reservoir. The Corps dismissed building the dam in the Green River Gorge because not enough water could be stored and dismissed building the dam in the upper river valley, because the reservoir would destroy salmon-spawning grounds. Three miles upriver from the Tacoma dam, work began in 1958 to span the sides of Eagle Gorge with an earth-filled dam 450 feet long and 235 feet high anchored into the volcanic bedrock.

Howard Hanson wasn't there when the dam began operations on Christmas 1961; he was honored posthumously by a congressional act renaming the dam after him. For $39 million—a million and a half coming from the state, half a million from the county, and the federal government paying for the rest—seven miles of the Green River and four miles of the North Fork of the Green River behind the dam would become a lake when winter runoff threatened flooding. The river was finally tamed.

To get its water, Tacoma in one stroke closed off half the 480 square miles of the watershed's river and tributaries to salmon and steelhead spawning and rearing with its 17-foot-high diversion dam. What thoughts might have been about the fish went the way of the fish trap and haul that was installed to take returning fish to the hatchery downriver but was soon abandoned.

Tacoma wanted clean drinking water and didn't want any fish upstream of their diversion dam. On the other hand, the U.S. Army Corps of Engineers and dam supporters said that a flood control dam would be good for the fish. The Howard Hanson Dam was authorized by Congress for the purposes of "first, flood control, and second, conservation by providing an augmented low water supply for the preservation of fish life." The river flows through a tunnel in the dam, and when it storms from November to March, the dam operators close off the tunnel and hold the river's flow in the reservoir and release the water in amounts that keep the river downstream tamely flowing to the Sound.

Beginning as early as March, the spring runoff is gradually collected in the reservoir, and the water is released through the fall in an amount that "assures a sufficient water level for successful fish migration and spawning, while enhancing sport fishing for steelhead trout, and coho and chinook salmon on the Green River and in Puget Sound," the U.S. Army Corps of Engineers' public information bulletin says. When the river flow gets naturally low in the summer and fall, there is usually enough water in the reservoir for Tacoma to take its 113 cubic feet per second and for the Corps to meet its guaranteed minimum flow of 110 cubic feet per second. It only gets tense when there isn't enough water because Tacoma has a senior water right to 113 cubic feet per second or all available water flowing in the river, which means, if Tacoma chose, it could dry the river up.

When the river was wild, the fish were healthy. When the river was tamed, the fish became less healthy. The Corps' public information brochure notwithstanding, every fisherman wants more fish and more opportunities to catch more fish. When there are less and less fish, the restrictions of who gets to catch which fish and when and how many become more stringent. Tensions naturally rise. In proposing a project that affects the river's water, project sponsors must now deal with the fish and the people who want the fish.

Tacoma has learned that lesson with its long-standing project first unveiled in 1963 to take an additional 100 cubic feet per second from the river, raise its headworks dam by six and a half feet, drill wells along

Dam construction at Eagle Gorge, site of the Howard Hanson Dam (photo courtesy of the Museum of History and Industry, Seattle)

the North Fork of the river, build a new storage tank next to the river, and build a second pipeline, Pipeline #5, to bring more water to Tacoma. Over the years, Tacoma has talked about the second diversion project as getting more water to meet its customers' needs and more recently as a regional system connecting its system with Seattle's and the South King County suburban water districts. Sending Tacoma water back to Seattle and King County cities would be sweet irony after ending up with the floodwaters of the White River in 1906.

In the 30-plus years since the project was announced, new players have entered the game. In 1974 the federal government began honoring its 1854 treaty with Northwest tribes by requiring that the state's fisheries be co-managed and equally shared by the state and tribes. After five years of negotiating with the Muckleshoot Indian Tribe, Tacoma reached a wide-ranging agreement in 1995 setting higher minimum instream flows before Tacoma could divert water, allowing the tribe access to the watershed, providing the tribe with cash and property settlements, and building a new salmon hatchery for the tribe. In exchange, the tribe agreed to drop any objections to the second diversion project.

"There's some measure of justice for the impacts Tacoma has had on this community, which includes the fish," says the tribe's Water Resources Program Manager Holly Coccoli. "Is the river better off? Certainly in the dry summer and fall. The new flow restrictions are better than the state's. I'd like to make a pipeline settlement that never hooks the pipeline up to the river, but that wasn't the reality."

In approving Tacoma's request for an additional 100 cubic feet per second diversion, the state required that the Corps' minimum flow of 110 cubic feet per second be increased to 150 cubic feet per second during summer and early fall at the river's first gauge at Palmer before any water could be diverted to Pipeline #5. The Muckleshoot Tribe did better by negotiating with Tacoma an increase to 200 cubic feet per second at the Palmer gauge and an increase to 300 cubic feet per second beginning in mid-September when chinook were spawning. At the Auburn gauge, they agreed to a flow of 400 cubic feet per second during the summer. If these amounts of water didn't remain instream, Pipeline #5 couldn't operate.

During drought years, the agreement between the tribe and Tacoma also establishes a requirement that at least 250 cubic feet per second flow through the downstream gauge at Auburn. In the severe drought of 1987, the river's flow dropped as low as 157 cubic feet per second at Auburn and chinook had their backs out of the water and couldn't move upstream over shallow gravel bars. Two-hundred-fifty cubic feet per second of flow would be about six inches more water in the river at Auburn. Tacoma agreed to curtail its diversion under its first water right of 113 cubic feet per second to guarantee that minimum flow, if necessary.

For Tacoma, the second diversion project still has a $190 million financing package it hopes to share with Seattle and South King County water districts and a pipeline to build. At the headworks, the U.S. Army Corps of Engineers proposes to expand reservoir storage and, with Tacoma, proposes to enhance the upriver fisheries and restore fish habitat. The Corps and Tacoma sometimes sound like fisheries managers who happen to control floods and sell water on the side. The proposal includes putting a thousand adult salmon above the Howard Hanson Dam, a far cry from the mid-1970s when Tacoma Water Superintendent John Roller protested vigorously when State Fisheries pushed to plant baby salmon above the dam. Roller painted a dire picture of salmon decaying in the drinking water and Tacoma having to install a $142 million filtration system. He sued to stop Fisheries and lost.

"The utility has changed," says Tacoma fish biologist Paul Hickey, who points to the hiring of a fish biologist as one indication of the change. "There's been a shift in thinking, and the evolution came during negotiating with the tribe. The water resource projects need to balance the natural and physical resources with our municipal water users' needs. Call it a voluntary choice driven by pragmatic need."

Pipeline #5 has become Tacoma's Green River Enhancement Proposal. It is a lightning rod for those who fish and boat and want not just more water but more water coming at the right time and in the right amounts. Tacoma's original Pipeline #5 Environmental Impact Statement in 1974 didn't even mention the impacts on recreational boaters, says Pat Sumption of Friends of the Green, a group that also reached a settlement agreement with Tacoma over the second diversion project.

"The problem with taking another 100 cubic feet per second of water out of the river is that you want 1,200 cubic feet per second, but you have to look at it on a kind of sliding scale because some boaters will boat it at 1,100," says Pat. "Some will boat it at 1,200 and others will boat it at 1,300, so how many days will you gain or lose with every 100 cubic feet per second you take out of the river? What we want is water in the river, and what we got was a recreation study to look at what the recreational boaters need in terms of flow and ways in which you can operate the dam so that you can get more water when you need it."

For the fish, the benefit of the proposal to increase storage at

Howard Hanson Dam is higher summer stream flows, but that also requires storing the river's water and reducing its flow earlier in the spring, which slows the flow of the river when smolts are moving out of the river and takes water away from the river's side channels. These lateral habitats are incubation areas, the gravel bar pools where juvenile chinook feed and grow on the bugs and nutrients slowly swirling in the river's backwaters. What, exactly, is good for the fish?

At a 1977 Seattle conference on Northwest electric power issues, aluminum industry attorney Roy Culp predicted that the disputes over allocating electric power will seem minor compared to the battles in the decades to come over who gets the water. The prediction seemed more fitting to the arid West of Mulholland and his successors, not the Northwest of the good rains.

The waters of the Green River flow down the heavily logged slopes of the upper watershed and pool behind dams before being piped to Tacoma, rafted on, spawned in, and allowed to flow to the inland sea. The flows and pollutants in its tributaries can be monitored, regulated, and bemoaned over openly. The main river's flows can be gauged, its allocations fought over, and agreements made. What can't be seen is much harder to understand.

In the Lake Washington and Cedar River watershed, the state has found that pumping water from wells along Issaquah Creek and the Cedar River has reduced stream level flows significantly since 1980, even when no additional groundwater withdrawals were allowed. The Department of Ecology in 1995 was faced with 62 applications from municipal and housing developments for groundwater withdrawals which, if approved, would increase the amount of groundwater taken by an estimated 17 percent.

That there is a relationship between the river that can be seen and the groundwater that cannot be seen is known; what that relationship is isn't really known. The "hydraulic continuity" has something to do with groundwater recharging the river and its tributaries, adding to their flow, and cooling their waters. Tacoma will pay for a "water use and availability" study for part of the Green River watershed as part of its settlement with the Friends of the Green and other river groups.

"Hydraulic continuity is a scientific fact," the state Pollution Control Board said in the summer of 1996 when upholding the Department of Ecology's denial of about 200 water right applications in areas such as the Lake Washington, Cedar River, and Green-Duwamish River basins. In these basins, more groundwater withdrawal might further lower stream flows already not meeting minimum flow goals. Building in the Covington Water District, which serves around 10,000 households, has been on hold until the district gets its permit to withdraw more groundwater. If you can't get more water, you can't build more houses—and developers around the region howled at the board's decision that put the burden of proof on them to demonstrate that withdrawing groundwater wouldn't impair stream flow. Some threatened to jump through a state loophole by clustering homes served by wells withdrawing less than 5,000 gallons of water a day and exempt from state permitting.

The story goes on, but it always returns to the river—a river and its land no longer in balance. The river's waters are dammed, turned off and on like a spigot, and allowed to flow channeled and rectified. The uplands are paved and built over; the rains that fall percolate less to groundwater, flow with more pollutants, and flood the tributaries. Groundwater is pumped to toilets plumbed for flushes that get treated and discharged into Puget Sound. The lowland valley soil is dewatered and compressed to pave and build over; the rains that fall become storm water bearing the multitude of civilization's residues that must be collected, filtered, and pumped away.

Many people have come to the river and its land in this time of gathering. Much has been taken from the land and its river; little has been given back. The many who have come have not understood the language of the river and its land. Few are those who understand and speak the language. They are the teachers and the new stewards of the land and its river.

Conclusion

WITH JOHN BEAL AT HAMM CREEK

IT'S EARLY SEPTEMBER at Point Rediscovery, on the middle fork of Hamm Creek where the waters from up around Des Moines find their way down through a culvert under a high bank and flow free for a while before disappearing into twin culverts 320 feet under Highway 99. On the east side of the highway, the creek runs free again in a drainage ditch for 1,000 feet, goes underground for 1,000 feet under the boat builders at Delta Marine, runs free for 300 feet, then goes underground for a final 120 feet before emptying into the Duwamish River.

What appears to be just another Duwamish industrial area drainage ditch, where the water goes thataway to the river, is now a remarkable example of a creek in balance, where the salmon now come thisaway, returning to the creek to spawn. Their offspring then follow the creek's flow thataway and return to the Duwamish River to begin their Pacific journey.

This is John Beal's creek, no doubt about it, even though King County today lists its restoration work here as an example of a new public stewardship. It's an uneasy partnership because what John's accomplished, he's done with his hands without money, and what the county does, it does with money and machinery. Disagreements are bound to arise about what's best for the creek and the fish, and sometimes John gets angry, sometimes he gets philosophical, but whatever he says is so full of love for the creek that you can agree or disagree or scratch your head puzzled, but you will never forget John Beal or Hamm Creek.

Today, John walks the creek:

"Thirteen years ago, I went to everybody—the Department of

Wildlife, Fisheries, King County, water districts—and said, 'Do you mind if I adopt Hamm Creek and try to bring it back to life?' Every single one said, 'John, it's impossible, it's a ditch, it's no longer a salmon stream, it's no longer a fishery. It doesn't have the ability to come back.' So, I said, 'Then you don't mind if I mess with it a bit?' 'Well,' they said, 'What do you plan on doing?' I said, 'I plan on taking out the garbage; I plan to clean the water wherever I can.' 'Well,' they said, 'Those are all commendable tasks, and we wish you well with it, but we can't help you remove the garbage, and we can't really help you financially.' Twelve years, long story short, we rebuilt an entire ecosystem that contains the ants, the gnats, the jiggers, the fox, the hawks, the nutria, the beaver, the muskrat—all of this has been brought back to a system that someone said was absolutely unhelpable.

"Right here, it was filled with about 12 old IBM computers, not PCs but the old terminals with big racks, thrown over the bank. There was a car sitting over in there, a refrigerator, a stove downstream, and the rest of the whole streambed was filled with tires and boots and just garbage. People are still dumping stuff over that bank, and in three years it will be down to the stream. Garbage has a three-year cycle. It gets dumped at the top, falls about six to ten feet in a year, falls another six to ten feet in another year, then finally ends up in the river. All by itself.

"Here's my first rock weir, and that's where I found Dietrich Hamm's initials—DH—written in German script. All of this over to the City Light Substation and down to Turn Basin Number Four was his until it was subdivided into Moore's five-acre tracts in 1951 because his wife needed money to live.

"It took me years to figure out where to put this rock weir. I figured it out by watching crawdads and how they built their rock lair so that the water coming over the top of the lair created a small sump, a sink, downstream. They live in their lair to rest and go back to the sump to eat what washes downstream and collects there. At normal flow, their sump was five feet back of their rock lair. At high water, that sump would be back seven feet because the water comes over their lair faster and washes farther down. Crawdads are aquatic creatures, basically the same as salmon, and I realized that if I placed the main rock weirs in the same configuration like the crawdads, it would work for the salmon. And it worked in the first year—it was incredible how it worked.

"The rock weirs create a deep spot downstream where the salmon can rest, get more oxygen to get up through the shallow water to the next weir's sump, and then to the next weir's sump. The rock weirs are

50 feet apart because that's the salmon's basic level of energy to get from one sump to the next. Now that's based on Hamm Creek's water flow; that won't work on Longfellow or Puget Creek. You have to do it to their water levels, and you would have to take the crawdad, place him in there, and he'll tell you where the weir should be. He's the best engineer in the whole world. I don't care who has gone to what college to learn this; if you use a crawdad, you'll find out exactly where to place your weirs and how to do it.

"The fish wait in the river until it rains. They won't return in low water because there's not enough water to get them up. And lo and behold, every time, nature provides the rain. The rock weirs keep the channel fairly clear, and the big important part I learned about rock weirs is that you need a center rock that will run your water from one side to another so there's enough water flow to get them to the next sump. Right here the channel's wider and the waters are very low, and they actually walk through the gravel to get to the next sump. As you go up a stream, the deepest sumps have to be at the top because the fish really need the respite. They've come through hell to get there. They are so tired when they reach this rock weir they will wait here for 45 minutes to an hour just ingesting oxygen and a little nutrition and getting a little more strength, and then they take off.

"This is where the steelhead and coho find their main respite before they go up to a fairly shallow channel and fairly high flow and a helluva fight to get to the culvert. The culvert's wide and has a slower flow, so they move right into that. Inside the culvert it's dark, a place for them to hide. Every fish—steelhead, cutthroat, coho, chinook—they'll get halfway in and stop and stay there for some time. Sometimes they won't have enough oomph to get upstream, and they'll come back down and spawn in this section, but most times they do.

"When I began this project, one of the things I was told was, 'Beal, you'll never bring fish here because they gotta go through a thousand feet of culverts to get here, and they'll never do that.' Well, I learned that if they've got a McDonalds waiting on the other end, they'll go through hell. Part of the culvert system's actually beneficial because it gives them a place where they know they're not going to be eaten. It's dark, they can rest. They're generally a nocturnal fish. If you look at wild salmon cycles, they feed at night and at dark periods. For so many years it was, 'Beal, you don't really have salmon in Hamm Creek. You buy them from IGA and put in carcasses, and the schools provide you with the young fish the next year.' That's because everybody who thought

I didn't have fish got off work at four o'clock. They didn't come out here at night, they didn't sit here at midnight and watch the fish runs. To understand, you gotta do things on the creek's time, not yours. That's part of the stewardship process I want to instill in people. You gotta take that extra step, maybe sleep in today and go out at midnight to see what's happening. It's a whole different place when it starts to get dark. Chickadees come out, grosbeaks come out, kingfishers will actually come out and fish.

"Here you've got blackberries, you've got alder, Indian plum, cottonwood. There's shade and cover where a lot of the spawning happens because it's not the main floor of the Kingdome. I've left vines of deadly nightshade. Swallows, sparrows, and chickadees eat it. Before King County cut down the cottonwoods, we had not hundreds but thousands of goldfinches coming here and breeding. Every tree would be alive with breeding pairs, and you'd look and see a sea of yellow and it was just wonderful. I've seen a few of them come back, but they won't stay.

"The goldfinches taught me the chain, the web. This was a niche, a place they came back to year after year, like the swallows return to Capistrano. The swallows' droppings provide them with their own food source. The goldfinches would come in and I'd have a day of beautiful thistle bloom, a blue, three- to four-foot canopy. Within two days, the flowers were gone, the seeds ingested and put back in their droppings— replanted before they left. It goes further. I found ants living on the thistles as well. The ants were a big part of the diet of the goldfinch. Without the thistles, we've lost a lot of our ant population. The chain, the web's been broken—seriously messed with. It's going to take me years to re-create this process. We need to bring in more ants. We need to plant more thistles, and then I'll plant the cottonwoods. If you look at a cottonwood, you'll see ants crawling up its trunk. They love the sap.

"Birds are the answer to a lot of prayers. They're an answer to re-seeding and keeping down the bug mass. It's just sad to see the whole cycle's missing now. This place used to be alive with birds, it was a place where local wildlife had a place to be. Without it, they've gone somewhere, but where have they gone? Was this their last niche? I don't know, but I've got a hunch that every time we lose a small niche, we lose a major part of the chain. Every time the small niches go down to development we think, 'They're not here anymore, but they're somewhere.' But are you sure of that? I'm not, and that's the scariest part. They're somewhere, but where is somewhere? No one can tell you.

"The fish will take care of the stream. The crawdads, the mayflies, the periwinkles will all find their niches within the stream if you have the process. That means that when the mayfly at a certain time in its cycle eats meats, you have to have jiggers and gnats that fall into the stream naturally and feed the process. Some ant varieties take their dead and store them for six months and every spring take those to the edge and throw them into the water. That feeds a lot of fish.

"I used to spend hours, days sometimes, digging up a nest to find the queen ant and enough of the little guys. One day, I had dug this nest down to my chest, and I thought, 'You get more bees with honey than with vinegar.' So first I tried a sugar solution, which didn't work because the ants drowned. Tried beer, but that didn't work. I put honey with basil in a jar and did it for three days, and on the fourth day, here's this queen and guardian ants out looking around. I swept her up, put her in a Mason jar, brought her over here, and put her in the hole. That summer I moved 18 colonies of ants. It was simple. You have to stay with it. Honey has an aroma, and basil actually adds to the aroma. You put your jar out in the morning and come back in the evening before it gets too dark and collect your ants. Because once it gets dark, they come out of the honey and go back into their nest. I also realized that if you bury the queen with the other ants, they are going to find their way out and the other guys will just follow them down the hole. It's worked every time since.

"I've brought back to the stream crawdads, periwinkles, mayflies, and other larvae. I've brought ants, I've brought jiggers, I've brought gnats. One year, I found a way to collect jiggers. I brought them back here and let them loose and tried to knock them into the water so the fish could eat them. That didn't work, and people thought I was really crazy. Well, that's the day I learned that what I had to do was take a creature and release it and monitor it until I can understand its life cycle. Jiggers will stay around the stream in the afternoon because of the cooling effect of the water, the same way they do in your backyard after you've watered your grass. Then they go into the forest and feed, and then they return. Their life cycle is about three weeks, and it seems a lot of them actually expire when they're hovering. When they're on the leaf resting, they'll naturally fall in. I realized that all I had to do was start with one brood and they'd proliferate throughout the year. Whenever the temperatures get to about 50 to 60 degrees, they find the trees, and they sit underneath the leaves to keep warm. When fall comes, they lay their eggs and they're gone. When spring comes, the eggs hatch and they're back, and you've got yourself another mix.

"I've brought in plants from wherever I could get them, and a lot of them were covered in aphids. So I brought ladybugs down here, but it was the wrong time of year, and they immediately went to the highlands to breed. The following year they came down, and in just these last couple of years, they've finally reached their cycle. They now come down at the normal times, they leave, and it's great because they're now part of the ecosystem. They taught me that my expectations are not necessarily what nature needs to have or to do. That taught me to wait, wait until next year, see what happens next week; mark and log this time and date in your log, and come back the next year looking. That's been my biggest learning curve. I go through my log every day, and I go back a week and go forward a week, and I see, 'Ah, gotta look for ladybugs next week.' That's exciting for me because I've got something to do, to really see, and when you see them, you realize that the cycle works.

"The most exciting time was bringing back the helicopter bugs, the dragonflies. I got four different colors from Bugs 'R' Us in Ballard, and I laid these colors out in a way so that I could determine which colors were coming back. Now the colors are mixing, and I'll see blue, I'll see green, a red one, a yellow one, all in the same vicinity, and I know that somehow they've been able to mix. They provide a tremendous fish feed when they lay their eggs in the water. Sculpins see a dragonfly laying eggs and they'll fall back to be right where the eggs are going to come down to the bottom and smoke 'em up. I didn't bring in sculpins, they came back naturally when the food resource was back. They've been a problem because they're predators, but they also eat the dead. Wild salmon will never, never take food from the bottom. Sculpins will. When I fed the fish here for two years, I was always concerned I was going to come down one of these days and find the whole stream smelling terrible. I never had that problem because the sculpins and the crawdads cleaned up. They're engineers at night.

"I've brought Indian plum back throughout the entire area, but my biggest and most intensive planting has been buttercup and the rye and fescue and asparagus grass. Buttercups absorb the oils, solvents, and soaps. I've done more asparagus grass because I've found out how to seed it. That stuff grows everywhere, but it wasn't growing here, and that wasn't natural. For the first two years, it was only a foot high, but now some of them grow up to six, seven feet. It's another natural bioremediator, and it really does an effective job.

"The other thing I brought in a lot of was clover. It's a tremendous feed resource for the ants and the gnats and the other critters because it's got nectar. But it's also a tremendous bioremediator of the soil, because when it falls back, it puts nitrogen in the soil. Cottonwoods would get this great surge of growth through that nitrogen fix, and I realized that the whole ecosystem includes the soil, too. The soil feeds that tree mass and what feeds the seed mass feeds the birds and the bugs.

"Everything is part of the balance. You know if the stream is in balance by looking at the rocks. Turn them over and see if there are larvae. These here are mayfly. See them move? That's a small periwinkle. That's the balance. That's what tells you that everything is in relation. Every rock must have at least one or two larvae, that rock has three or four. When you get into an area where you don't have any, you know that you're out of balance, and it's that simple. I'm proud that you can pick up any rock in this stream and it's going to have some sort of larvae on it. And this time of year is when your larvae are really down. Spring is when they really flourish. Still, throughout your winter process, you have to have a larval stage to know you are still in balance. That's what brought me to biocheck.

"Biocheck is a boom filled with cotton and wrapped in an outer layer of nylon mesh I lay across the stream. I put amoebae bacteria on the mesh, and they live in the cotton, which I fill with compost soils and plants. The roots grow in the boom, absorbing oils, soaps and detergents, and solvents as a nutrient, converting them in an organic process. The plants fall back in winter but the boom continues to collect seeds during the winter, so the next spring, plants are growing in the boom again and beginning the process over.

"Now it's low water and we're coming into the heavy rain period, so it's primarily soaps that need to be removed by the biocheck boom. The entire upper valley is filled with old septic systems, and the soaps and detergents we now use come down the stream as bubbles, get stopped by the biocheck boom, and the plants and bacteria eat them. The oils right now are not too bad. With biocheck, I've reduced the stream's oil content by about 70 percent. The time when oils enter my stream now is after a rain and the water's running off the roads. But the reed canary grass, the asparagus grass, the buttercups, and especially the Indian plum absorb the oil as a nutrient. Indian plum runs its roots right to the water and will turn black with oil in the spring and summer high rains. The plant flourishes and actually gets a little hit off the oil, which gives it a natural antifreeze. They will die back after the third or fourth really severe frost, but they last longer, which gives me a little better overgrowth, better larvae content.

"Upstream of the biocheck boom, you'll find a certain amount of larvae. Below biocheck, you'll find double that, three times the amount. Every single time. The most important part for anybody who is trying to monitor or maintain a stream is to go in once a week, the same day, every week, 52 weeks out of the year and take your rocks out and find your larvae. If you don't find any, you know you have a problem, and you have to find out what your problem is. What's killing the larvae? The easiest way is to put the rocks in a simple solution of alcohol and water, and if you find oils coming to the surface, that's your problem. You'll also find out very quickly if soaps or detergent are your problem. In a normal pristine mountain stream, the stream purifies itself by running across rocks and minerals. In an urban stream, the rocks are laden with the chemicals that beset the stream, so you're not purifying at all. People don't see the rocks, they look at them every day, but they don't see the rocks. I didn't either until I saw the fish eat from the rocks.

"It's a very small creek, it's a ditch, it's a trickle. Yet this year over a million salmonids left the stream. Out of just this trickle. Think of what could be done with Newaukum and Soos Creeks. Lord. But here is the potential of people understanding that through stewardship, a long-term commitment, these systems can all come back. The key is the rocks. Start with the rocks and work out."

Amen.

Bibliography

Auburn Argus. Various articles: November 15, 1906; January 5, 1907; January 12, 1910; April 8, 1911; April 11, 1914; November 13, 1914.

Blomberg, George, Charles Simenstad, and Paul Hickey. "Changes in Duwamish River Estuary Habitat Over the Past 125 Years." *Proceedings of the Puget Sound Water Quality Authority Puget Sound Research Conference,* 1988.

Blood, Tom. "Environmentalist Restores Self While Restoring Waterways." *Beacon Hill News/South District Journal,* March 6, 1996.

Buerge, David. "Longacres: The Golden Years." *Seattle Weekly,* August 19, 1992.

Buerge, David. "Requiem For A River." *Seattle Weekly,* October 16, 1985.

Chittenden, Hiram Martin. "Report of an Investigation by a Board of Engineers of the Means of Controlling Floods in the Duwamish-Puyallup Valleys and Their Tributaries in the State of Washington." Lowman, Seattle, 1907.

Churney, Marie and Susan Williams. *Bogs, Meadows, Marshes & Swamps* Seattle: The Mountaineers, 1996.

Collier, Phyllis. "The Sands of the Black River Are Shifting." *Seattle Post-Intelligencer,* April 27, 1980.

Dodge, John. "Saving the Salmon." *The Olympian.* Special Report 1994–1995.

Doughton, Sandi. "Even Brief Exposure to Pollution Harms Fish in Sound, Study Finds." *The News Tribune.* June 21, 1992.

Flewelling, Stan. *Farmlands: The Story of Thomas, A Small Agricultural Community in King County, Washington.* Auburn, Wash.: Eric Sanders Historical Society, 1990.

Forsman, Leonard. "History of Western Washington Native Peoples." In *A Time of Gathering, Native Heritage in Washington State,* edited by Robin K. Wright. Seattle: Burke Museum–University of Washington Press, 1991.

Hanson, Howard. "More Land For Industry." *Pacific Northwest Quarterly,*

January 1957.

Isaacs, Gary et al. "Special Duwamish River Studies." Water Quality Series No. 1, Municipality of Metropolitan Seattle, February 1964.

Jerry V. Jermann, et al. *Continued Archeological Testing at the Duwamish No. 1 Site.* Office of Public Archeology, Institute of Environmental Science, University of Washington Reconnaissance Reports No. 11, Seattle: March 1977.

Jones & Jones, Landscape Architects. *A River of Green and Technical Appendices*, prepared for King County Deptartment of Planning and Community Development. Seattle: Jones & Jones, Landscape Architects, 1979.

Jones, LeRoy. "Where Have All the Farmers Gone?" *Pacific Search*, March 1975.

King County Planning Commission. "Duwamish Valley Study Area: Renton, Kent, Auburn." 1957.

King County Surface Water Management. "Habitat Sites in the Duwamish/Lower Green River: A Self-Guided Tour." Seattle, 1995.

Knappen-Tippetts-Abbett-McCarthy. *Development plan for Duwamish and lower Green River Valley*, prepared for Duwamish and Green River Joint Survey Board representing City of Seattle, King County, Port of Seattle, 1954.

Kruckeberg, Arthur. *The Natural History of Puget Sound Country*. Seattle: University of Washington Press, 1991.

Langloe, Lars. "Report on Development of Industrial Sites in the Duwamish-Green River Valley." Prepared for the Seattle Planning Commission, September 1946.

League of Women Voters of King County. "Farm For Sale: A Study of King County Farmland Preservation." June 1977.

Livingston, Vaughn. *Geology and Mineral Resources of King County, Washington*. State of Washington Department of Natural Resources, Bulletin No. 63, Olympia, 1971.

Manning, Harvey. *Footsore 1: Walks and Hikes Around Puget Sound*, 3d ed. Seattle: The Mountaineers, 1988.

Manning, Harvey. *Footsore 4: Walks and Hikes Around Puget Sound*, 2d ed. Seattle: The Mountaineers, 1990.

Matsuda, Robert I. et al. "Fishes of the Green-Duwamish River." Water Quality Series No. 4, Municipality of Metropolitan Seattle, Seattle, December 20, 1968.

Metro. "Moving in the Right Direction: A Progress Report on Water Quality in the Duwamish River, Elliott Bay and Central Basin of Puget Sound." Municipality of Metropolitan Seattle, April 1994.

Moore, Milo and Don Clarke. "Report on the Fisheries Resource of the Green-Duwamish River." State of Washington Department of Fisheries and Department of Game, March 1947.

Ott, John. "The History of Tacoma City Water and the Belt Line Railway." In *The Tacoma Public Utilities Story*. Tacoma Public Utilitities, 1993.

Pryne, Eric. "Troubled Waters." *Seattle Times*, June 17, 1992.

Scott, K. M., P. T. Pringle, and J. W. Vallance. "Sedimentology, behavior, and hazards of debris flows at Mount Rainier." Washington: U.S.Geological Survey Open-File Report, 90-485, 1992.

Seattle Post-Intelligencer. "The River That Disappeared." August 8, 1982.

Seattle Post-Intelligencer. Various articles: November 15, 1906.

Seattle Times. "A History of Horse Racing in the Puget Sound Area." June 16, 1996.

Seattle Times. "A River Forgotten." March 18, 1981.

Slauson, Morda. "Where Was The Black River?" Renton Historical Society, 1967.

Tanner, Curtis. "Potential Intertidal Habitat Restoration Sites in the Duwamish River Estuary." Prepared for The Port of Seattle and the United States Environmental Protection Agency, 1991.

United States Army Corps of Engineers. "Green and Duwamish Rivers and Duwamish Waterway, Seattle Harbor, Wash." Letter from the Secretary of the Army transmitting a letter from the Chief of Engineers, United States Army, dated February 28, 1949, submitting a report on a preliminary examination and survey of the Green and Duwamish Rivers and a review of reports on the Duwamish waterway authorized by the Flood Control Act approved on July 24, 1946 and requested by a resolution of the Committee of Rivers and Harbors, House of Representatives, adopted on April 18, 1946.

United States Army Corps of Engineers and Tacoma Public Utility. "Proposal for the Howard Hanson Dam Additional Water Storage Project." February 9, 1996.

Valley Daily News. "Salmon May Slow Soos Creek Development." July 7, 1989.

Washington State Department of Ecology. "1996 State Water Quality Assessment: Section 305(b) Report." No. WQ-96-04, June 1996.

Washington State Parks and Recreation Commission. "The Green River Gorge: A Conservation Proposal." Olympia, November 1968.

White River Journal. Various articles: June 25, 1898; September 15, 1900; September 22, 1900.

About the Author

Mike Sato is Communications Director of People For Puget Sound, a 20,000-member grass roots organization educating and involving people in the protection and restoration of Puget Sound and the Northwest Straits. Since the group's launch in late 1991, he has been responsible for all print and electronic communications, media and community relations, and membership development.

Mike's understanding of the Puget Sound environment and the people shaping that environment also comes from his work as the first public information officer for the Puget Sound Water Quality Authority. He has also done extensive work in the electric utility industry as public information coordinator for Seattle City Light and corporate communications director for Hawaiian Electric Company and Hawaiian Electric Industries. A graduate of Reed College, he began writing professionally in 1977, publishing and editing weekly newspapers in the San Juan Islands and Seattle.

Other titles you may enjoy from The Mountaineers:

DEAD RECKONING: Confronting the Crisis in Pacific Fisheries, *Terry Glavin*
An intriguing, in-depth account of the West Coast's dwindling fish populations and the perilous state of the Pacific fisheries.

TREE HUGGERS: Victory, Defeat, and Renewal in the Northwest Ancient Forest Campaign, *Kathie Durbin*
A timely account of the high-profile campaign to preserve the Northwest's ancient forests. Award-winning journalist Durbin offers the most up-to-date history available.

IMPRESSIONS OF THE NORTH CASCADES: Essays about a Northwest Landscape, *John C. Miles*
A diverse collection of original essays explores Washington's North Cascades. Thirteen contributors interpret different facets of the North Cascades from the perspectives of their disciplines and daily experiences.

THE ENDURING FORESTS: Northern California, Oregon, Washington, British Columbia, and Southeast Alaska, *Ruth Kirk and Charles Mauzy*
The landscapes and ecosystems of the ancient forests are brought to life through full-color photographs and the text of five regional authors in this large-format tribute. Co-published by The Mountaineers Foundation.

CHRONICLING THE WEST: Thirty Years of Environmental Writing, *Michael Frome*
Collection of articles by nationally known environmental journalist Michael Frome documents the most urgent environmental issues to have confronted the Western United States over the past three decades.

NISQUALLY WATERSHED: GLACIER TO DELTA: A River's Legacy, *David George Gordon and Mark Lembersky*
Seventy color photographs and text profile this model watershed.

THE MOUNTAINEERS, founded in 1906, is a nonprofit outdoor activity and conservation club, whose mission is "to explore, study, preserve, and enjoy the natural beauty of the outdoors. . . ." Based in Seattle, Washington, the club is now the third-largest such organization in the United States, with 15,000 members and five branches throughout Washington State.

The Mountaineers sponsors both classes and year-round outdoor activities in the Pacific Northwest, which include hiking, mountain climbing, ski-touring, snowshoeing, bicycling, camping, kayaking and canoeing, nature study, sailing, and adventure travel. The club's conservation division supports environmental causes through educational activities, sponsoring legislation, and presenting informational programs. All club activities are led by skilled, experienced volunteers, who are dedicated to promoting safe and responsible enjoyment and preservation of the outdoors.

If you would like to participate in these organized outdoor activities or the club's programs, consider a membership in The Mountaineers. For information and an application, write or call The Mountaineers, Club Headquarters, 300 Third Avenue West, Seattle, Washington 98119; (206) 284-6310.

The Mountaineers Books, an active, nonprofit publishing program of the club, produces guidebooks, instructional texts, historical works, natural history guides, and works on environmental conservation. All books produced by The Mountaineers are aimed at fulfilling the club's mission.

Send or call for our catalog of more than 300 outdoor titles:
The Mountaineers Books
1001 SW Klickitat Way, Suite 201
Seattle, WA 98134
1-800-553-4453
e-mail: mbooks@mountaineers.org